LIFE
MOBSTERS AND GANGSTERS

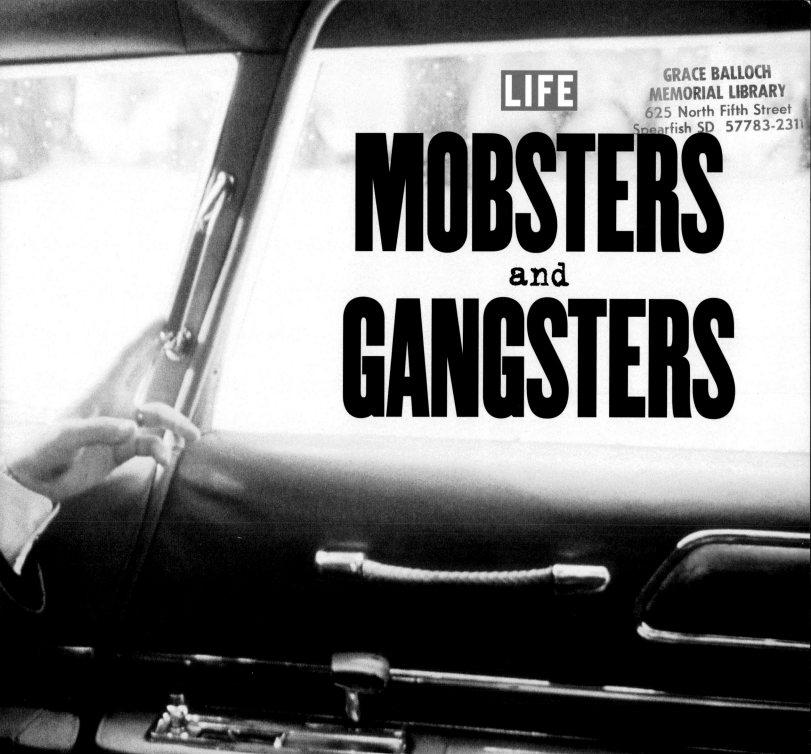

LIFE
MOBSTERS
and
GANGSTERS

Organized Crime
in America,
from Al Capone to
Tony Soprano

LIFE

Editor Robert Sullivan
Creative Director Ian Denning
Picture Editor Barbara Baker Burrows
Executive Editor Robert Andreas
Associate Picture Editor Christina Lieberman
Assistant Picture Editor Vivette Porges
Senior Reporter Hildegard Anderson
Writer/Reporters Lauren Nathan, Rachel Silverman
Copy J.C. Choi (Chief), Stacy Sabraw
Production Manager Michael Roseman
Picture Research Lauren Steel
Photo Assistant Joshua Colow
Consulting Picture Editor (London) Suzanne Hodgart

Publisher Andrew Blau
Director of Business Development Marta Bialek
Finance Director Camille Sanabria
Assistant Finance Manager Karen Tortora

Time Inc. Home Entertainment

President Rob Gursha
Vice President, Branded Businesses David Arfine
Executive Director, Marketing Services Carol Pittard
Director, Retail & Special Sales Tom Mifsud
Director of Finance Tricia Griffin
Marketing Director Kenneth Maehlum
Assistant Director Ann Marie Ross
Prepress Manager Emily Rabin
Associate Book Production Manager Jonathan Polsky
Associate Product Manager Jennifer Dowell

Special thanks to Suzanne DeBenedetto, Robert Dente,
Gina Di Meglio, Anne-Michelle Gallero, Peter Harper,
Michelle Kuhr, Natalie McCrea, Jessica McGrath,
Mary Jane Rigoroso, Steven Sandonato,
Bozena Szwagulinski, Niki Whelan

"Crime Does Pay" by Elmore Leonard first appeared in LIFE
in November 1990. Reprinted by permission of the author.

Published by

LIFE Books

Time Inc. 1271 Avenue of the Americas, New York, NY
10020

Library of Congress Control Number: 2002106439
ISBN: 1-929049-84-6

"LIFE" is a trademark of Time Inc.

We welcome your comments and suggestions about LIFE
Books. Please write to us at: LIFE Books, Attention: Book
Editors, PO Box 11016, Des Moines, IA 50336-1016

If you would like to order any of our hardcover Collector's
Edition books, please call us at 1-800-327-6388. (Monday
through Friday, 7:00 a.m.–8:00 p.m. or Saturday, 7:00
a.m.–6:00 p.m. Central Time).

Please visit us, and sample past editions of LIFE,
at www.LIFE.com.

Half Title Legs Diamond, 1937 PHILIP LEVINE/N.Y. DAILY NEWS

Previous Pages Al Pacino as Michael Corleone
in *The Godfather II*, 1975 KOBAL COLLECTION/PARAMOUNT

Right Police escort Machine Gun Kelly
from a Memphis jail, 1933. BETTMANN/CORBIS

LET'S GET ORGANIZED

In the 19th century, rules were being established and boundaries being drawn for a nation within the nation: Gangland, U.S.A.

Jacob A. Riis Collection/Museum of the City of New York

Before there was organized crime in America—the particular subset of nefariousness that we will deal with in this book—there was disorganized crime pretty much everywhere. In considering only the largest of natural-law offenses like, say, murder, the discovery of petroglyphs and old bones tells us that Native Americans and European hunters were afflicting one another with criminal intent long ago, whether or not there was any written code of conduct. Ancient Rome must have broken every rule in the prostitution-rape-and-incest category, and the Bible is full of stories regarding thieves, redeemed or otherwise, as well as white-collar crimes among moneylenders. It is safe to say that, ever since Adam shared the apple with Eve, the human condition has had a criminal element.

If we take a global rather than strictly domestic view, it becomes evident that even crime of the organized kind has a long if not necessarily noble heritage. The word "thug" dates to early 13th cen-

According to an 1888 account in the *New York Sun*, denizens of this alley in lower Manhattan known as Bandit's Roost seemed "calculated in appearance and character to keep up the appropriateness of that name."

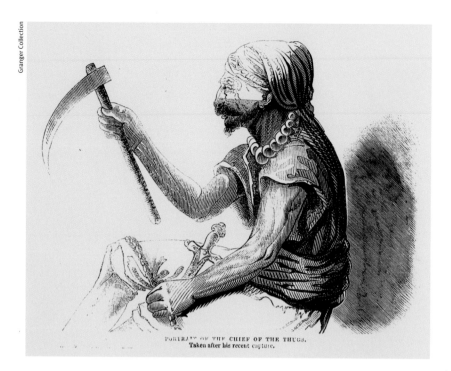

PORTRAIT OF THE CHIEF OF THE THUGS.
Taken after his recent capture.

But if Prohibition was the catalyst for organized crime in America, it was not the starting point. Well before gangsters took up tommy guns, their philosophical forebears were brandishing Colt .45s out West, while their urban kinsmen were prowling slums with cheap gats or baseball bats. These miscreants moved as teams, often against other teams, and that's what organized crime is all about.

The wild, wild West was thick with freelance criminals, true, but it also had its gangs—James-Younger, the Daltons, Butch Cassidy's Wild Bunch—whose approach to horse thievery and bank robbery was as organized as any homicidal sociopath could devise. Even further back, there was Samuel Mason and his band of not-so-merry men. Their career in southern Illinois serves as a nice starting point for organized crime in the incorporated United States. Mason had been an officer in General Washington's Continental Army. After his discharge he established, in 1797, a rustic tavern called the Cave-in-Rock on a scenic bluff overlooking the Ohio River. Mason's minions would move upriver to guide or aid pioneers, luring them to the hollow outside the cave where they were relieved of their possessions and, frequently, their lives. The Mason Gang thrived into the early 1800s when it was supplanted at the cave by an outfit headed by the Harpe Brothers, escaped murderers from Kentucky.

The Mason and Harpe operations, with their careful scheming and a desire to perfect a plan of

tury India, when Thugz, or gangs of criminals, roamed from town to town, looting and pillaging. Smuggling and drug-trafficking rings are as old as the hills in Asia and Africa, and extant criminal organizations in Italy and Japan trace their histories back several centuries. The Mafia came together as a secret society in Sicily in the late Middle Ages. Its original goals might have been political, concerned with protecting the island's locals from foreign invaders such as Normans and Spaniards. However, the Sicilian mob's civic altruism was short-lived, and for several centuries it has been a vigorously criminal enterprise.

Today, of course, the United States is—as in so many other areas—a world leader in organized crime. How did this come about?

Prohibition, which lasted from 1920 to 1933, certainly didn't hurt. Organized criminals are often wont to traffic in desirable commodities, licit or not. Today's cravings for heroin or cocaine, no matter how keen, are minor addictions compared with America's thirst for bathtub gin during the Roaring '20s. Gangsters of all pinstripes got into the game of manufacturing or distributing bootleg hooch; many mobsters from the burgeoning U.S. branch of the Mafia came out in brutal force. When the 18th Amendment was repealed at last, organized crime shifted its focus to other going concerns, including, but not limited to, loan-sharking, extortion, illegal gambling, labor racketeering and drug smuggling.

This Indian Thug has disguised himself as a traveler's escort by painting the upper half of his face white. Illinois's Cave-in-Rock was, in the early days of the Republic, a den of thieves and murderers, disguised as a riverside tavern.

In the 1860s young Frank (left) and Jesse James brandish their pistols. By the 1870s, Jesse (below, far left) had grown so proud and brazen, he invited a photographer to the gang's Missouri hideout to create a historical record.

attack and use it over and over, can be seen as prototypes for the outlaw gangs of the West. Among the most famous and successful was that led by brothers Frank and Jesse James, along with Bob, Cole and Jim Younger. The James boys learned lessons in psychopathic violence from a true pro when they rode with Confederate guerilla William Quantrill during the Civil War. After the war, they joined with the Youngers in a decade-long crime career that began with a $60,000 bank robbery in Liberty, Mo. The James-Younger gang ultimately killed 21 in the course of netting almost half a million dollars from banks and trains. The Youngers were caught in 1876; Jesse James was shot in the back by gang member Bob Ford in 1882 (an early instance of gangster mutiny); and Frank James surrendered to authorities, then was acquitted of his crimes. He lived out his life as a farmer.

Whether the Daltons would have succeeded in Coffeyville on October 5, 1892, had they narrowed their focus to just the Condon Bank (above) is doubtful; the bullet holes and pockmarks show that the town delivered a furious fusillade that day. Below: The gang poses posthumously.

Another set of brothers, Bob, Emmett, Gratton and Bill Dalton of Coffeyville, Kans., were devotees of the James-Younger gang, and set out to emulate their idols in 1890. Bob led a team, whose shifting roster often included Arkansan Bill Doolin, on a series of train heists. In 1892, Bob planned a major assault on his own hometown. Wearing disguises, five gang members tried to rob two banks simultaneously but were met in the street by a barrage of bullets. The Daltons killed four, although Bob and Gratton were also cut down, along with two of their men. Emmett survived only to be jailed.

Bill Dalton and Bill Doolin didn't ride into Coffeyville that day, but they rode together throughout the Oklahoma Territory during the next couple of years, robbing trains and banks as they went. The Doolin-Dalton gang lost half of its leadership when a posse killed Dalton in 1894. The same fate befell Doolin two years later.

The last of the old-time western gangs was the Wild Bunch, led by a Mormon bishop's grandson, one Robert LeRoy Parker of Beaver, Utah. He would be better known as Butch Cassidy, an alias taken in honor of Mike Cassidy, a tutor in cattle-rustling. Butch was a precocious outlaw, barely 20 when he

TOM EVANS,   BOB DALTON,   GRAT DALTON,   TEXAS JACK,

joined the McCarty Gang, whose coleader, Bill McCarty, was said to have ridden with the Jameses. Jailed for horse theft in 1894, Cassidy formed his own gang after being released in 1896. The Wild Bunch specialized in bank and train robbery, and featured a lineup of all-star criminals whose nicknames set the colorful tone for generations of gangsters to come: Kid Curry (né Harvey Logan), the Tall Texan (Ben Kilpatrick) and, yes, the Sundance Kid. This last was Harry Longabaugh of Wyoming, and he and Butch made a dashing, fascinating pair. "I have never killed a man," Butch once claimed, and it may have been true. A crack shot, he was known to aim for the legs of horses rather than at pursuing lawmen. Sundance was renowned as one of the finest marksmen in the West, but he, too, was slow to draw. When affairs got red-hot for the Wild Bunch in 1901, Butch and Sundance, along with

The Wild Bunch was not averse to cleaning up for the camera lens. Cassidy commissioned a formal portrait of his gang after a successful bank job, then sent a copy to the bank (Butch is seated at right, Sundance at left). The Kid and Etta pose in New York before fleeing in 1901.

After years of rampant lawlessness in the West, the law fights back. Above: A team of rangers on the Union Pacific is prepared for the Wild Bunch. Left: In 1890 a quarter million dollars in gold departs Homestake Mine in South Dakota with four Wells Fargo guards attendant.

the Kid's girlfriend, Etta Place, decided to flee rather than fight. They made for Argentina, where they ranched in peace until 1906. At that point, Pinkerton detectives picked up their trail, so Butch and Sundance, perhaps figuring that since they were being treated like criminals they might as well act like criminals, reverted to their bank-robbing ways. It is probable that they were killed by soldiers after a robbery in Bolivia in 1908, though legend has the duo returning to the U.S. under aliases, then enjoying serene retirements in the West.

The appearance of Pinkerton agents in the Wild Bunch story shows that, as crime was getting better organized, so was crime-fighting. In Chicago in 1850, Scotsman Allan Pinkerton established one of the first U.S. detective agencies and gained an early reputation by breaking up a counterfeiting ring. In 1861 he formed and headed the U.S. Army's secret service division, even while his own agency was amassing the country's largest and most useful store of information about criminal activity. "Pinkerton Men" were hard guys, and when they weren't breaking heads for union-busting industrialists in the East, they were hounding run-amok gangs in the West. In 1868, Pinkerton agents captured the train-robbing Reno Brothers outfit, offering early proof that detection and doggedness were more effective in fighting crime than hastily formed civilian posses.

FORM 55-3-'01-10M-AE.

P. N. D. A *AP* **No.**

NAME......George Parker.　　No. 469 R
ALIAS......"Butch" Cassidy; George Cassidy; Ingerfield.
NATIVITY...United States.　COLOR......White
OCCUPATION...........:......Cowboy; rustler
CRIMINAL OCCUPATION..........Bank robber, highwayman, cattle and horse thief
AGE......37 yrs (1902).　HEIGHT.....5 ft. 9 in
WEIGHT....165 lbs....　BUILD.......Medium
COMPLEXION...............　......Light
COLOR OF HAIR.........................Flaxen
EYES..........Blue.　NOSE....................
STYLE OF BEARD.....Mustache; sandy, if any
REMARKS:—Two cut scars back of head, small scar under left eye, small brown mole calf of leg. "Butch" Cassidy is known as a criminal principally in Wyoming, Utah, Idaho, Colorado and Nevada and has served time in Wyoming State penitentiary at Laramie for grand larceny, but was pardoned January 19th, 1896. Wanted for robbery First National Bank, Winnemucca, Nevada, September 19th, 1900 See Information No. 421.

FORM 55-3-'01-10M-AE.

P. N. D. A *AP* **No.**

NAME......Harry Longbaugh.　No. 470 R
ALIAS......"Kid" Longbaugh; Harry Alonzo; Frank Jones; Frank Boyd; the "Sundance Kid"
NATIVITY..Swedish-American.　COLOR..White
OCCUPATION..............　.....Cowboy; rustler
CRIMINAL OCCUPATION.........Highwayman, bank burglar, cattle and horse thief
AGE......35 years.　　HEIGHT.......5 ft, 10 in
WEIGHT......165 to 175 lbs.　BUILD. ...Good
EYES....Blue or gray.　NOSE.....Rather long
COMPLEXION...........................Medium
STYLE OF BEARD..........Mustache, (if any), natural color brown, reddish tinge
FEATURES............................Grecian type
COLOR OF HAIR....Natural color brown, may be dyed; combs it pompadour
IS BOW-LEGGED; FEET FAR APART.
REMARKS:—Harry Longbaugh served 18 months in jail at Sundance, Cook Co., Wyoming, when a boy, for horse stealing. In December, 1892, Harry Longbaugh, Bill Madden and Henry Bass "held up" a Great Northern train at Malta, Montana. Bass and Madden were tried for this crime, convicted and sentenced to 10 and 14 years respectively; Longbaugh escaped and since has been a fugitive. June 28, 1897, under the name of Frank Jones, Longbaugh participated with Harvey Logan, alias Curry, Tom Day and Walter Putney, in the Belle Fourche, South Dakota, bank robbery. All were arrested, but Longbaugh and Harvey Logan escaped from jail at Deadwood, October 31, the same year. Wanted for robbery First National Bank, Winnemucca, Nevada, September 19th, 1900. See Information No. 421.

The sophisticated techniques of Allan Pinkerton (left) changed the game. Among his agency's innovations was the dissemination of cards like these featuring Butch and Sundance—modernized WANTED posters. (Pinkerton might have thanked Butch for that studio portrait, from which these headshots were lifted.)

Strategies, guns, florid nicknames, organized opposition: The Old West wrote a thorough primer for mobsters and gangsters. There were even the standard accoutrements. Belle Starr, for example, can be seen as the very model of the modern major moll. Myra Belle Shirley's family allowed the James-Younger gang to stay at its Texas farm after the Liberty raid, and in due course 18-year-old Belle gave birth to a daughter, Pearl. Cole Younger was only the first in Belle's series of outlaw lovers, some of whom became her husbands. In 1866 she married Jim Reed, who would go on to a career of murder, stagecoach robbery and counterfeiting before being

Women of the West: In 1887, Belle Starr poses with firearms. A bit later, Doolin gang lookouts Anna McDoulet and Jennie Stevens, a.k.a. Cattle Annie and Little Britches, do likewise. The law caught up with the teens in '95.

gunned down in 1874; in 1880 she married Sam Starr, whose clan ran rustling and bootlegging operations in the Indian Territory west of Fort Smith, Ark.; after Starr was killed in 1886, Belle fell for Bluford "Blue" Duck, a Cherokee murderer. "I am a friend to any brave and gallant outlaw," said the Bandit Queen, who would bribe or seduce a lawman to keep her pals in circulation. She met her own end violently, felled by a shotgun blast to the back on February 3, 1889. Her son Ed was a suspect, as was her latest lover, a Cherokee named Jim July, but no one was ever indicted in her murder. "I regard myself as a woman who has seen much of life," Starr once said, hitting the target square.

As mentioned earlier, not all of organized crime's prehistory in this country was written left of the Mississippi. In fact, had the Irish boyo William Bonney, a.k.a. Billy the Kid, not gone west as a youngster, he would surely have thrown in with one of the ferocious gangs that infested the slums of his native New York City. The first of the famous Irish hoodlum organizations was the Forty Thieves, begun in the 1820s and run by Edward Coleman. They operated out of the back room of Rosanna Peers' Center Street grocery/speakeasy and dabbled in everything from pickpocketing to murder. The gang even organized a school system, training youngsters in the Forty Little Thieves how to bur-

gle. An orphan named Wild Maggie Carson head-ed the Little Thieves for a time, then was saved at age 13 by the Reverend L.M. Pease, who mentored her until she was adopted by a good family.

The Forty Thieves, who initially had the notori-ous acre-square Five Points District pretty much to themselves, quickly found themselves with worthy rivals as new Irish gangs formed both in the neigh-

In 1842, Charles Dickens wrote of the vile Five Points slum: "Debauchery has made the very houses prematurely old."

borhood and slightly uptown. Principal among these were the Bowery B'hoys, described by one his-torian as "ready for a lark, eager for a spree, reck-less of consequences and unreckoning of the future." Mose the Bowery B'hoy was said to be eight feet tall and able to tear a lamppost from the side-walk and wield it as a weapon. Statistics tell Mose's tale. He once killed 100 men in a day, he could sat-

In the late 1800s the muckraking photojournalist Jacob A. Riis went among New York gangs, including the Short Tails (top, right) and the Montgomery Guards (opposite). At one point, Riis asked for a demonstration of a mugging, and the gangsters above complied, "searching the victim's pockets with a deftness that was highly suggestive."

isfy 12 women at a time, he could swim across the Hudson River in two strokes (and could leap across the East River to Brooklyn), he smoked two-foot-long cigars, and he celebrated his street-fighting victories by downing four quarts of oysters, one barrel of soup, a dozen chickens, one pig and one steer, brains included. He washed down the whole with a barrel of coffee.

Mose probably never existed; he is the Paul Bunyan character of early gangland history. But his presumed presence was useful to the very real Bowery B'hoys in dissuading the Chichesters, Roach Guards, Plug Uglies, Short Tails and Dead Rabbits from Bowery turf. The B'hoys eventually bequeathed to New York such successor gangs as the True Blue Americans, the American Guards, the O'Connell Guards and the Atlantic Guards, as well as several politicians and a hit play, *Mose the Bowery B'hoy,* which opened at the Olympic Theatre in 1848.

In the latter half of the 19th century, perhaps the most vicious street gang in New York, also Irish, was the Whyos, said to be named for its members'

birdlike call. The Whyos—among them louts such as Red Rocks Farrell, Bull Hurley and Baboon Connolly—claimed all Manhattan as their domain, and killed in every sector. In fact, Mike McGloin, the primo Whyo in the early 1880s, decreed that a real Whyo must have committed at least one murder. Not inclined to preach what he did not practice, McGloin killed a saloon keeper with a slingshot in 1883. He was hanged, beginning a tradition among upper-echelon Whyos. Two Dannys who were reputed to be the greatest Whyos ever, Lyons and Driscoll, took over the gang in 1887 and not long thereafter came to similar grief. Danny boy number one, Driscoll, killed a prostitute named Beezy Garrity and met the hangman in January 1888. Lyons murdered Joseph Quinn, his rival for the affections of Pretty Kitty McGown, and followed his compatriot to the gallows in August of the same year.

The Whyos specialized in murder but were capable of other offenses. In fact, they published a guide to their services. When Whyo Piker Ryan was pinched in 1884, the police found in his pocket a

menu ranging from "punching" ($2) to "both eyes blacked" ($4) to "ear chewed off" ($15) to "shot in leg" ($25) and, yes, "doing the big job" ($100 and up). Although the Whyos were presumably adept at all they offered, the cases of McGloin, the Dannys and Piker demonstrate that they weren't all that hot at staying either alive or at liberty. By the early 1890s the Whyos were defunct, most members dead or behind bars.

The Whyos probably left the stage in the nick of time, as transitional gangsters Edward "Monk" Eastman and Paul Kelly were about to usher New York's underworld from its scruffy beginnings into a mature middle age. Brooklynite Eastman could not make a go of the pet shop that his father staked him to but found considerable success as a bouncer at New Irving Hall, a dance palace–cum-dump in Manhattan. His face took an awful beating in near-constant fights—rival gangsters nicknamed him Monk after his simian mug—but the other fellas got worse. His club had 49 notches on it one evening when he brought it down on the skull of an unobtrusive patron sitting at the bar. Asked why, as he carved another nick into the stick, Eastman replied, "I just wanted to make it an even 50."

The Eastmans, surely the greatest exclusively Jewish gang in New York City history, included many dandies and smooth operators who would prosper in crime—men such as Arnold Rothstein, the storied gambler and sports fixer. But their boss was a tough who punched out his prostitutes and never doffed his brass knuckles even when he had an army of underlings to do his bidding. "I likes to beat up a guy every now and then," said Eastman. "It keeps me hand in." Eastman's strong-arm work sent so many men to the hospital that a ward in Bellevue was nicknamed the Eastman Pavilion. Inevitably, his successful rackets enterprise was to butt up against that of Paul Kelly's Five Pointers.

Names are misleading in this case: Kelly was not Irish, and neither was his gang. "Five Pointers" was probably chosen to invoke dread by association. Kelly's name was chosen because boxers went by Irish monikers at the time, and boxing was Paulo Antonio Vaccarelli's trade—before he became a crime boss.

With the prize money he won as a ban-

Mike McGloin

Bull Hurley

Danny Driscoll

Piker Ryan

tamweight fighter in the 1890s, Vaccarelli/Kelly bought an interest in several Little Italy whorehouses. From prostitution he moved to storefront athletic clubs, which served as headquarters for young gangs that he consolidated under the Five Pointers banner. Eventually, Kelly's roster included more than 1,500 foot soldiers and was involved in all manner of crime, from petty larceny to election-fixing for Tammany Hall pols.

Eastman began encroaching on Kelly's territory, the situation deteriorated, and war was imminent. When Five Pointers went to crash an Eastman-sponsored crap game in August 1903, a massive gun battle broke out under the Second Avenue El. Hundreds of gangsters rushed to the area and fought it out for more than two hours, while fearful cops stayed at bay. Two Five Pointers were killed and five wounded; the Eastmans' toll was one dead, two wounded. Tammany Hall, faced with the worst gang fight in New York City history, tried to broker a crime-world truce, but it proved tenuous. Eastman proposed settling matters with a boxing match, and Kelly agreed. The two bosses staged another two-hour battle in a makeshift ring in a Bronx saloon and finally settled, exhausted, on a draw.

What might have happened in the great gang war between the Eastmans and Five Pointers became moot when Eastman, again roaming out of his territory, impulsively decided to mug a man in midtown. He was chased down by a Pinkerton detective, and this time Tammany threw him over, allowing the judge to impose a 10-year sentence.

Kelly now had the field to himself and he seized it, building a crime empire that he presided over in tuxedoed splendor from his headquarters at the New Brighton club on Great Jones Street. He set a tone and style that was admired and emulated by his young subordinates, who included Terrible Johnny Torrio, Lucky Luciano and Al Soon-to-be-Scarface Capone. It would be a short evolutionary leap for the Five Pointers to become the ultrapowerful "family" syndicates, and an equally short span to the Golden Age of mobsters and gangsters.

Two footnotes to the Eastman saga: A few years after his release from prison, he enlisted for service

Kelly's mug (above) survived the gang wars in better shape than Eastman's (below), although both leaders were happy to go to the front lines with their men. Kelly felt he was setting a good example for younger Five Pointers by being an active participant. Monk, well, Monk just wanted to have some fun.

in World War I and came home a hero, having unleashed his violent tendencies on enemy machine-gun nests. But when he tried to resurrect his crime career as a Prohibition Era bootlegger, the Five Pointers, still thriving, said that enough was enough. Eastman was iced in December 1920.

There was pre-Prohibition action in cities other than New York, to be sure. New Orleans was a near rival in the late–19th century importation of Italian mobsters, and when 19 members of a Sicilian gang were acquitted in the 1890 assassination of police superintendent David Hennessy, angry citizens took matters into their own hands, broke into the parish prison and hanged 11 of the accused men. In Chicago, such as Torrio were hanging out shingles, getting themselves organized. But it was in New York that the seeds were sown and traditions begun for mob rule, even as out West, gunslingers on horseback were paving the way for jalopy-riding gangsters like Ma Barker and Bonnie and Clyde. By the beginning of the Roaring '20s, the prologue for organized crime in America had been written.

And then, some very, very nasty characters turned the page.

THE PUBLIC ENEMIES

In the Roaring '20s, gangsters let loose in the inner city and across the heartland, running booze, breaking into banks, bumping each other off and battling the feds.

The American underworld is an incestuous place, and disentangling the DNA of mobsters and gangsters is about as easy as convincing a shylock to forgo the vig. While the Mafia in Sicily had clear definitions, rules and traditions—you're not going to find a lot of Lanskys and Siegels hanging with that rogues' gallery—its American counterpart has, pretty much from the start, been less ethnically segregationist and, in fact, only one part of the larger syndicate operation.

There's been cross-pollination from the get-go. As we have seen, such as Arnold Rothstein, Al Capone and Lucky Luciano got their training in the organized crime operations of turn-of-the-century New York before striking out on their own. To sketch just a few associations between them and some of the hoods to be dealt with shortly, Al Capone hired Baby Face Nelson and tried to hire Alvin Karpis. Rothstein used independent agent Legs Diamond as a leg-breaker, while doing daily business with syndicate chieftains Luciano, Frank Costello and Meyer Lansky. Legs also worked for Little Augie Orgen, who also employed Lucky. When Mafia boss Salvatore Maranzano wanted to put out a contract on

Luciano, Capone and a few others, he went to trigger-happy Irish thug Vincent "Mad Dog" Coll. In the criminal house of representatives, mobsters and gangsters were constantly crossing the aisle.

Having said that, a useful if fuzzy distinction can be drawn between a gangster and a mobster. Dedicated freelancers like Bonnie and Clyde and Machine Gun Kelly wouldn't have known Sicily from Siberia, and theirs is the picture next to the word "gangster" in the dictionary. Several other Prohibition-era independent contractors, although organized in their approach to criminal activity, were anything but mobbed-up; Dillinger, Diamond and Pretty Boy were not family men. Even Scarface Capone was far more gangster than mobster, happy to rule Chicago while watching his old cohorts plot and scheme and build their families brick by brick in New York.

The Golden Age of the Gangster coincided precisely with Prohibition, then faded as the syndicate—the American Mafia and attendant or affiliated organizations—said emphatically: You're in or you're out. If you were out, you were butting in, and therefore you didn't exist, at least not for long.

The Public Enemies, by contrast, existed—larger than life.

The quintessence of the American gangster, John Dillinger had a magnetic quality that obtained even as he robbed and murdered.

Arnold Rothstein

New York's preeminent underworld figure of the Roaring '20s and the years just before was Arnold Rothstein, the progenitor of organized crime in America. The man who would come to be known as Mr. Big was born in Manhattan in 1882, the son of a successful, philanthropic merchant. When Arnold's brother Harry said he would pursue rabbinical studies, his father was thrilled and said to Arnold, "You should be proud of being a Jew." Arnold shot back, "Who cares about that stuff? This is America, not Jerusalem. I'm an American. Let Harry be a Jew." Preferring the ambience of the pool hall, Arnold quit school, even though he was a math whiz. His obsession with figures was such that he played a lifelong game in which people called out numbers and he instantly performed calculations. His pal Nicky Arnstein once warned him to lay off the computations. "It just isn't good for you, A.R. It isn't normal and you'll hurt your brain."

It was those smarts, however, that took Rothstein to the top of the heap. His motto was "Treat the sucker right, he is paying your salary." Mob legends galore came under his tutelage. Luciano, Lansky, Costello and Torrio learned that the bottom line was what mattered, not the ethnicity of the people you teamed up with. He arranged for Louis Lepke Buchalter to become the honcho of the New York labor rackets. When Rothstein had a problem with a collection, he rang up Legs Diamond.

A.R. was the model for both Nathan Detroit in *Guys and Dolls* and Meyer Wolfsheim in *The Great Gatsby,* which brings us to the Black Sox scandal of 1919, when the Chicago White Sox threw the World Series. Legend has it that Rothstein fixed the outcome, but biographer Leo Katcher claims otherwise. "Rothstein's name, his reputation, and his reputed wealth were all used to influence the crooked baseball players. But Rothstein, knowing this, kept apart from the actual fix. He just let it happen."

Mr. Big, whose idea of a lovely evening was to walk down Broadway and savor the adulation of others, made millions from bootlegging, drugs and gems. His passion, though, was gambling, and it proved his undoing. In September 1928 he was in a three-day poker game hosted by George "Hump" McManus. For some reason, Rothstein, who never smoked or drank, had of late been acting erratically. During the game, he lost nonstop, until he was down $322,000. Shockingly, he left without paying up, saying he would come across in a day or two.

The next night he announced over dinner at Lindy's: "I don't pay off on fixed poker." Days turned into weeks . . . the heat was on Hump to get the money. On November 4, Rothstein took a call from McManus, who asked to meet him at the Park Central Hotel. There, Rothstein was shot in the gut. He died two days later. McManus was acquitted.

The case was never solved, but it is possible that Lansky and Luciano ordered the murder. With Rothstein gone, they stood to gain as they moved ahead on his idea for a national syndicate. Ironically it was Luciano who said of Rothstein, "He taught me how to dress . . . how to use knives and forks and things like that at the dinner table, about holdin' a door open for a girl. If Arnold had lived a little longer, he could've made me pretty elegant."

Rothstein makes an appearance at the New York State Supreme Court in 1928. Known as the Big Bankroll, he was also a master of the Big Fix. Addicted to gambling, Rothstein boasted that he would wager on anything but the weather. That was the one and only thing he could not rig.

The Purple Gang

I n 1957, Elvis Presley had one of his biggest hits, "Jailhouse Rock," which included the lyrics: "The drummer boy from Illinois went crash, boom, bang/The whole rhythm section was the Purple Gang." We don't know if songwriters Jerry Leiber and Mike Stoller were suggesting that the guy from Illinois who went "bang" was Al Capone, but there's no doubt about those deadly denizens of Detroit.

No good account exists of how they came to be called the Purple Gang, but the rest of their saga is clear. It starts out just before World War I and mainly involves the sons—the Bernstein and Fleisher brothers, Irving Milberg and Abe Axler stand out among many—of Russian Jewish immigrants. In a familiar pattern, an impoverished neighborhood was the breeding ground for minor offenses like bullying merchants, which soon escalated to rougher sorts of strong-arming.

When Prohibition arrived, Detroit's criminal element were already seasoned bootleggers, since Michigan had banned the sale of alcohol two years earlier. Canada was just a boat ride away in summer, and in the winter the Detroit River froze over. So brazen was the Motown bootleg biz, there was even a pipeline between an Ontario distillery and a Detroit bottler. The city now found itself with two flourishing economies, cars and booze.

The cutthroat world of illegal whiskey was heaven-sent for the Purples, who were hardly criminal geniuses or organized in any productive way but were, rather, venal roughnecks who never changed their style. They took over back-alley stills and muscled in on speakeasies and blind pigs. They hijacked liquor shipments and kidnapped other reprobates for ransom. They got a nice boost in 1925 with the inception of the notoriously vicious Cleaners and Dyers War, which would endure for several years. Corrupt launderers led by Sam Polakoff and Sam Sigman paid the Purples a grand a week to keep recalcitrant competitors in line, which meant murder, bombings and beatings,

exactly what the gang did best. Then, when the Sams wanted to terminate the deal, the Purples terminated them instead.

Big money had combined with ruthlessness to render the gang invincible; none dared testify against them. From 1927 to 1932, they reigned over Detroit's vice, gambling and drugs. Their stranglehold on booze was such that, as author Paul Kavieff says in *Off Color,* even "Capone thought it more prudent to make the Purples his liquor agents rather than go to war with the gang." The FBI would have liked to stop them, of course, and on one Yom Kippur, agents disguised themselves as Hasidic Jews at a Detroit temple. The ploy failed when the feds went outside to have a smoke, which was decidedly not kosher on a holiday.

Unable to alter their brutish ways, the Purples bit the dust one by one, either killed or exiled to prison for absurdly public crimes. In total, the gang murdered 500 people. By the mid-1930s, the Sicilian mob had moved in for good—adding Detroit to its big family.

Abe Axler, left, and Eddie Fletcher try to suss out what went wrong after one of their arrests. When Lucky Luciano's men entered Motown in the mid-'30s, these two were found bullet-riddled in the backseat of a car.

Pretty Boy Floyd

He was thought of as a 20th century version of Jesse James and called the Most Dangerous Man Alive. Charles Arthur Floyd was born in Georgia in 1904, but his impoverished parents soon moved him and his six siblings to Oklahoma. Before long, drought and pestilence drove the family into the bootlegging business. Still, things continued to be tough, prompting Floyd to hold up a post office. He made off with $350 in pennies, and the die was cast. In 1925 he began serving a three-year stretch for robbery, and one year after being released he was arrested in Toledo for a bank heist. He was on a train headed to a 12-to-15-year term in the state pen when he jumped out a window and escaped.

By this time, Floyd had acquired the nickname Pretty Boy from Beulah Baird, a procuress who often consorted with him. With a variety of partners he robbed banks across the Midwest and back in Oklahoma, where some considered him a hero since he occasionally destroyed mortgages in those banks, even as he took the loot.

On the morning of June 17, 1933, Floyd and two others, trying to free a pal, shocked the nation when they killed four peace officers as well as the prisoner in what was called the Kansas City Massacre. Thereafter, Floyd was doggedly pursued until, on October 22, 1934, local cops and FBI agents led by Melvin Purvis cornered and shot him on an Ohio farm. The police carried him to the shade of an apple tree, where he died. He had on him $120 and a watch and fob. The timepiece had 10 notches carved on it—one for each man he had killed.

They took Floyd's body to Sallisaw, Okla., and buried him in a plot he had selected a year earlier. At that time, Pretty Boy had told his mother, "Right here is where you can put me. I expect to go down soon with lead in me, perhaps the sooner the better. Bury me deep."

At top, Floyd poses for the police in 1931. Pretty Boy was always impeccably groomed, courteous and never wore a mask, even as he robbed banks in broad daylight. At left, a fingerprint session at the East Liverpool, Ohio, morgue, in 1934.

John Dillinger

The most famous of all American bank robbers, Dillinger differs from many other superstar criminals in that he doesn't seem to have been a full-throttle psychopath, at least not at the start. He was no Andy Hardy, to be sure, but there was a dignity to the man, despite his bloody calling.

John Herbert Dillinger was born in Indianapolis in the month of June, in either 1902 or 1903. His mother, Molly, died when he was three; his father, Honest John, was a grocer, alternately strict and permissive with his boy. Young John was intelligent but quit school early and took a menial job. After an unhappy love affair, he stole a car, and to avoid jail time enlisted in the Navy, only to jump ship a few months later.

Back in Indiana and up to no good, he was arrested for assault and attempted robbery. He took his father's advice and pleaded guilty. After all, he had no record and his family was in good standing in the community. When he heard the sentence, he was devastated: 10 to 20 years in the state pen.

He would serve nearly half that time, much of it in solitary and the rest learning at the knee of career criminals how to rob banks. When he was paroled in May 1933, he was an angry, resentful man, and things were about to go haywire. Within months he was picked up for robbing a bank in Ohio. While he was in the pokey, some of his old prison friends—whose earlier escape he had masterminded—showed up, shot the sheriff and freed the prisoner. The Dillinger Gang was in the act of forming, and on its way to $300,000 from 11 bank robberies and a grand total of at least 15 deaths.

To the newspapers, the violence seemed incidental, as Dillinger was portrayed as cunning and affable, a kind of Robin Hood who stole from the same institutions that were foreclosing on broken farmers. The legend was galvanized in early 1934. After being nabbed for the murder of a policeman, Dillinger was being held in the Crown Point, Ind., county jail. With a wooden pistol he had whittled

Dillinger (above, in an Indiana courtroom), was doing time in 1933 when he wrote a letter to his father. He said, "I know I have been a big disappointment to you but I guess I did too much time, for where I went in a carefree boy, I came out bitter toward everything in general."

and blackened, he bluffed his way past a dozen guards, locked them up and fled in the sheriff's car with a couple of machine guns. The incident made headlines around the world.

Dillinger became the first person to be called Public Enemy No. 1. He underwent plastic surgery, adopted the alias Jimmy Lawrence and went to Chicago. There, he befriended a waitress named Polly Hamilton, who had a roommate who called herself Anna Sage. She was a native of Romania and was feeling heat from Immigration owing to convictions for pandering. Sage tipped off Melvin Purvis of the FBI that the three were going to see *Manhattan Melodrama,* a movie in which Clark Gable becomes a gangster. As they walked out of the Biograph Theatre, on July 22, 1934, the feds looked for Sage's red dress ("the Lady in Red") and shot and killed the outlaw. There is a theory afoot today that it wasn't really Dillinger who was shot but a petty criminal, and that Dillinger went off to Oregon. It seems unlikely, however, that he would suddenly change his spots and stop robbing banks. This was, after all, one gangster who didn't need a fancy nickname. He was Dillinger.

Bettmann/Corbis

Baby Face Nelson

Even in a milieu as violent as that of the gangster, there must be one whose fury outstrips all the others. Meet Lester Gillis. The son of poor Belgian immigrants, he grew up in the grotesque sanitation-canal district of Chicago. Lester's brothers and sisters managed to follow the straight and narrow, but the wee, angelic-faced Lester had an unerring nose for trouble. He was a flailing little fiend who would take on anyone, whether they asked for it or not.

Lester roamed the streets with other urchins, rolling drunks and robbing stores, his switchblade ever at hand. His cronies called him Baby Face. (In later life, very few dared utter the name in his presence.) While in his early teens, he was nabbed for car theft and sent to the Chicago Boys Home. Released after two years, he was quickly back for a couple more after breaking into a department store.

Back on the streets, he went into the "protection" business, selling "insurance" to pawnshops and brothels. It wasn't long before his particular skills attracted the attention of Al Capone, who hired Baby Face as an enforcer. He got the job done, to be sure, but soon enough his tommy-guns-and-baseball-bats approach rankled the labor unions. Capone relied on union backing, so Big Al and Baby Face parted ways.

It was time to earn money on his own again, and armed robbery seemed a natural to the five-foot-four, 133-pound maniac. He made $5,000 robbing a gems dealer just before Christmas in 1930, but was caught holding up a bank a month later. He had served a year at the Joliet pen when he was removed to stand trial on another charge. On the return trip, he overcame the guards and escaped.

Car and bank robberies marked his trail west. He changed his name to George Nelson and in 1934 joined the Dillinger outfit. The FBI learned that the gang was vacationing at the Little Bohemia Lodge in Wisconsin. In a nocturnal fiasco, the feds shot three civilians, while Nelson killed two agents and a constable. After a bank job that same year, he shot two cops dead outside of Chicago.

When FBI director J. Edgar Hoover then released the Public Enemies List—Dillinger at

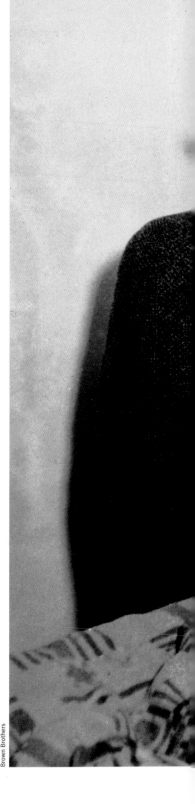

Brown Brothers

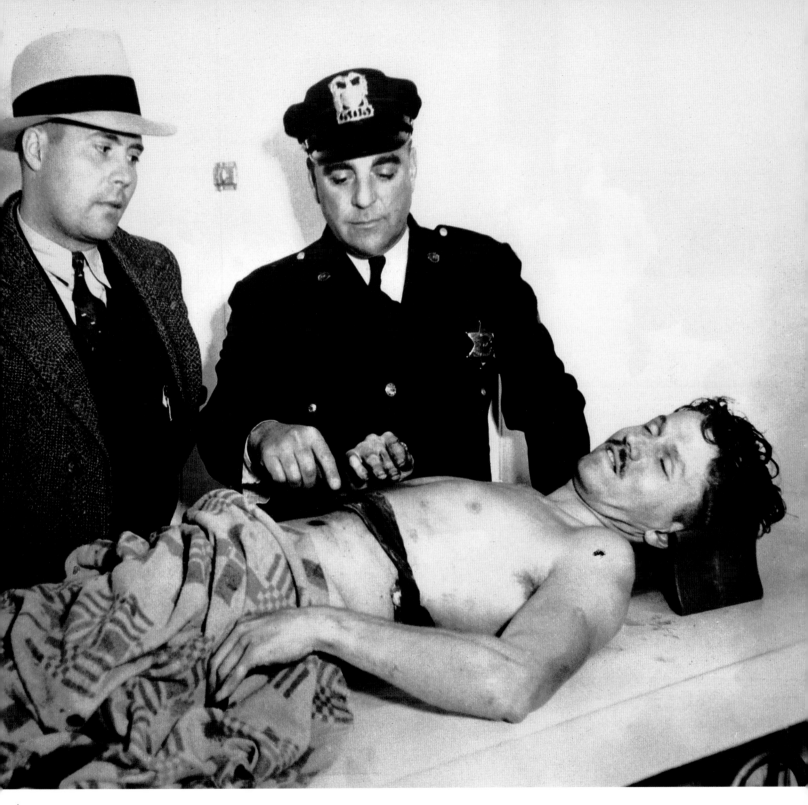

No. 1 with a $20,000 bounty, Nelson runner-up with $10,000 on his head—Baby Face was incensed: "Don't these lawmen know they are dealing with the most dangerous man in America?" After Dillinger was killed in July 1934, Nelson rose to the top spot, but the press said he didn't measure up to Dillinger. Said Nelson, "Even if I have to rob a bank a day, they'll see who's the best."

Five months later, federal agents discovered Nel-son driving a stolen car in Barrington, Ill. Gunfire rang out, and Nelson pulled his car over to bring the matter to a head. "I've had enough of this cat and mouse," he cried. Advancing on the feds, tommy gun blazing, he was hit by 17 bullets, but killed two agents. A highway worker at the scene said, "It was just like Jimmy Cagney." Baby Face, who had often bragged that he wouldn't be taken alive, died that night at age 25.

In the Cook County, Ill., morgue, the police chief and an officer examine the wounds. They were among several lawmen who wanted to be photographed with Public Enemy No. 1.

America's favorite crime couple style for the camera in 1933. It may be noted that they didn't stray far from their car, which in '34 was hit by 167 bullets.

Bonnie and Clyde

I n an era rife with gaudy criminals, Bonnie and Clyde stand out as a double-barreled powerhouse, short-lived, but with at least a dozen corpses strewn along the wayside. They were both born in small Texas towns and came of age in Dallas. Both were small (she stood four foot 10 and weighed 85 pounds), and both bore strong family ties right up to their grisly end. But other than a fervent love for each other—and a flair for publicity—they were quite different.

Bonnie Parker was high-spirited, popular and a good student, excelling in reading and writing. Her father was a mason, and her mother stayed home, tending to her three kids. It was a normal family, though the father died young. When she was 16, Bonnie married her high school boyfriend, Roy Thornton, a bad apple whom Bonnie broke with after a couple of years. In 1930 she moved to Dallas, where she was a waitress and "bored crapless."

Clyde Barrow's father was an illiterate sharecropper, and the family were squatters. Clyde quit school in the sixth grade, left home and soon was stealing cars and holding up stores with his brother Buck. In 1930 he visited an injured friend who was being taken care of by none other than Bonnie Parker. The two clicked, and for Bonnie, boredom would cease to be a concern.

Before long, Clyde was arrested for burglary and sentenced to two years in a Waco jail. Bonnie then entered the realm of crime when she strapped a revolver between her breasts and smuggled it into Clyde, who escaped, was recaptured and sent down to Eastham Prison Farm, an indescribably brutal hellhole where he did two years of seriously bad time and became a seriously hard man.

Reunited in 1932, Bonnie and Clyde set off on a crime spree across the Southwest (they never liked to venture too far from

their families back in Texas), terrorizing small banks and businesses. Sometimes brother Buck was with them, along with others, but Bonnie and Clyde were inseparable. Authorities uncovered and released photos of the duo, including one of Bonnie with a pistol in her hand and a cigar clenched in her teeth. The publicity further inspired lawmen to bring them in, dead or alive.

It would, of course, be dead. On May 23, 1934, they were driving a stolen Ford in Louisiana when a six-man posse led by former Texas Ranger Frank Hamer ambushed them and fired 50 bullets into the desperados, ripping them to pieces. Clyde, who had one lens of his sunglasses shot out, was ID'd by a missing toe that he had once cut off with an axe in a failed ploy to get out of jail. Bonnie, who was wearing a red dress, red shoes and a red-and-white hat, was ID'd by a tattoo on her upper thigh. Said Hamer, "I hate to bust a cap on a woman, especially when she was sitting down. However, if it hadn't been her, it would have been us."

Houston Chronicle

Mad Dog Coll

On October 6, 1931, two days after he was arrested for the "Baby Killer" shootings, Coll appears in a New York courtroom. He had dyed his blond hair black to evade the huge manhunt.

The "Mad Mick" burned briefly but white-hot in the latter Prohibition era. Before he was through he would need a couple of other monikers to better describe his accomplishments. The archetypal Irish American hooligan of the time, Vincent Coll grew up in the aptly named Hell's Kitchen area of New York City. He was a malevolent child, prone to flashes of ruthless violence. By his teens he was expert with guns and had been a participant in several slayings. A stint in the reformatory served only to provide him, upon release, with a job as a gun-wielding rum-runner for Dutch Schultz.

Coll saw the money there was in booze, and he told Schultz he wanted in on the profits. Schultz ixnayed that, so Coll, with his brother Peter and others, started his own operation, which included hijacking the Dutchman's beer trucks. On May 30, 1931, Schultz had 24-year-old Peter Coll gunned down in the street. In the ensuing gang war, some two dozen hoods were killed.

In July, Coll and a couple of his soldiers tried to rub out Schultz's right-hand man, Joey Rao, on a crowded Spanish Harlem street. Rao and his crew ducked for cover, but an infant in a baby carriage and four other children were wounded. A five-year-old boy died. Everyone knew Coll had done it, even if he said, "I'd like nothing better than to lay my hands on the man who did this. I'd tear his throat out." Coll walked on the charge, but remained known in the press as "the Baby Killer."

At about this time, Mafia chieftain Salvatore Maranzano was deciding to put out a contract on such heavies as Lucky Luciano, Vito Genovese, Frank Costello and Joe Adonis. Since no one in his right mind would take on such a suicidal job, Maranzano turned to Coll, who immediately accepted a $25,000 down payment. Coll was on his way to begin his work when Maranzano himself was killed; it seems that Luciano had been tipped to Maranzano's intentions. Coll dropped his assignment, though he did keep the cash.

Eventually, the battle with Schultz caught up with Coll. On February 8, 1932, the 23-year-old bigshot hoodlum now known as "Mad Dog" walked into the London Chemists' Shop on West 23rd Street to carry out business on the pay phone. A man entered, walked up to the booth and opened fire with a tommy gun, killing Coll instantly. The next day, the proprietor of the store assured newsmen that rather than hurt his business, the murder had increased it, as people flocked to see the Baby Killer.

In a delicious tie-in, it turns out that newspaper writer Walter Winchell had, on the very day of Coll's murder, written in his column: "Five planes brought dozens of machine gats from Chicago Friday to combat The Town's Capone. Local banditti have made one hotel a virtual arsenal and several hot spots are ditto because Master Coll is giving them the headache."

Legs Diamond

Nobody is sure how Jack Diamond got his nickname. Some say that as a young hood he always outran the cops. Others say he earned it on the dance floor. Yet others contend it was because he always ran out on his friends. No confusion, however, surrounds his other moniker, the Clay Pigeon of the Underworld. He survived so many shootings that even he began to believe he was bulletproof.

The product of a Philly slum, he moved to New York in 1913 at the age of 16, and he and his brother joined a gang of thieves called the Hudson Dusters. Jack was starting to get noticed by the big shots when he was drafted in 1918. But this was no military man, and he promptly went AWOL. Charged with desertion and stealing from his "buddies," he served a year and a day in Leavenworth.

Following his release, he worked as a bodyguard for Arnold Rothstein and became a bootlegger for Little Augie Orgen, who also employed such as Lucky Luciano, Louis Lepke Buchalter and Waxey

Gordon. From then on, it was the big time for Legs Diamond, which meant oodles of money, dames, arrests, gunshot wounds and homicides, most notably at his Broadway speakeasy, the Hotsy Totsy Club, whose back room was the last place a lot of men ever saw.

The big time also meant seething feuds, especially with Dutch Schultz. For two years, they scrapped over the booze trade. When they finally met and agreed to a truce, Dutch's top aide was slain as he left the building. In retaliation, Dutch killed Legs' brother, Eddie.

On December 18, 1931, Legs celebrated beating yet another felony rap with his wife and friends at a speak in Albany, N.Y. After a while he left and spent a few hours with his longtime mistress, showgirl Kiki Roberts. Then he went to a boarding house, where he passed out. Soon, outside, two men got out of a long black car, climbed the stairs, and as one held Legs' ears, the other put three soft-nose bullets into the back of his head. The killing was never solved, and Legs certainly had as many enemies as anyone, but the finger pointed mainly at Dutch Schultz, who had once groused, "Can't anybody shoot that guy so he won't bounce back up?"

Legs wears a here-we-go-again look for the 1930 Philadelphia mug shots at top, but displays his jauntier side during a stroll the following year.

The Barker Gang were equal-opportunity robbers—banks, payrolls, post offices. They also killed and kidnapped. At left, Ma and Alvin Karpis. At top right, Doc feels lousy in the Ramsey County, Minn., jail on January 9, 1935. A week later, Fred and Ma lay side by side in Florida.

Ma Barker and Alvin Karpis

Arizona Donnie Clark was born in 1872 in the Ozark Mountains of Missouri. Once, as a child, she was thrilled to glimpse one of the area's celebrated personalities, Jesse James. Later, she herself would become the 20th century's most infamous female gangster—Ma Barker. Yet she remains a shadowy figure.

The Ma Barker Gang, which tore up the Midwest in the 1920s and '30s in a maelstrom of kidnappings, murders and robberies, included three of her sons, Fred, Herman and Arthur. When the boys were young, Ma left her husband and moved them to Tulsa, where they and several other misfits burgled and robbed as the Central Park Gang. As the brothers grew, the crimes became more serious.

Ma's loyalty to her sons was already legend when, in 1927, she suffered a tremendous blow. Herman was stopped by two policemen concerning a stickup. He shot one in the head, but fearing capture he killed himself. Ma would never be able to accept that her oldest son would commit suicide. She was bereft and, for a time, alone. Arthur—better known as Doc—was serving a life sentence for murder, while Fred was doing five-to-10 in the state pen. There he would make a friend who would take the Barker gang to bigger and worse things.

Alvin Karpis was born in Canada in 1908 and raised in Topeka, where he took to crime like a leopard to a three-legged goat. Described as "supersmart," Karpis once said, "In another set of circumstances, I might have turned out to be a top lawyer or a big-time businessman or made it to any high position that demanded brains and style, and a cool, hard way of handling yourself." Al Capone thought Karpis was aces and tried to hire him, but Karpis didn't want to get involved with organized crime. No reflection on Scarface, however, whom Karpis considered "a wonderful person . . . a real man."

Karpis and Fred Barker were set free in 1931 and immediately set off on a spree, albeit one methodical in approach and execution; Karpis's photographic memory was instrumental in planning. Doc was pardoned in '32 and fit right in, along with other recruits. As the murders, kidnappings and thefts mounted, the FBI feverishly tried to stop the headline-grabbing rampage. Karpis recalled going to the movies with Ma and Fred once when a special presentation came on featuring pictures of "Dillinger, Baby Face Nelson, Doc, Freddie and me. The punch line was, 'Remember, one of these men may be sitting beside you.' The lights went on in the theater. The audience looked around and giggled."

The wild party started drawing to a close in January 1935 as G-man Melvin Purvis surprised Doc outside his Chicago apartment. When Purvis dis-

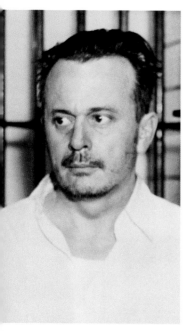

covered that Doc wasn't armed, he asked where his gun was. Said Doc, "Home, and ain't that a hell of a place for it?" (He would die four years later trying to escape from Alcatraz.) Later that month, Purvis and his crew approached a resort cottage in Oklawaha, Fla. Fred and Ma, holed up inside, let fly with machine-gun fire, triggering a six-hour battle. The agents found the mother and her son dead.

The operation was finally extinguished in May 1936 when Alvin Karpis, who held the title of Public Enemy No. 1 longer than anyone else, was located in New Orleans by FBI agents. J. Edgar Hoover went there to make the collar himself. "Creepy" Karpis would serve 32 years in federal prisons. He died in Spain in 1979, 10 years after being paroled.

The Barker Gang was surely one of the vilest criminal enterprises in American history. But what about Ma? When she died, she was called the brains of the outfit. Today, there is room for doubt. Karpis himself wrote in 1971, "It's no insult to Ma's memory that she just didn't have the brains or know-how to direct us on a robbery. It wouldn't have occurred to her to get involved in our business . . . We'd leave her at home when we were arranging a job, or we'd send her to a movie. Ma saw a lot of movies."

Where did the notion of a female monster come from? Some say the FBI. When Ma was shot, the last thing the agency wanted was to have killed an old woman with no criminal record, so Hoover saddled her with a persona. "The eyes of Arizona Clark Barker always fascinated me," he once said, interestingly. "They were queerly direct, penetrating, hot with some strangely smoldering flame, yet as hypnotically cold as the muzzle of a gun."

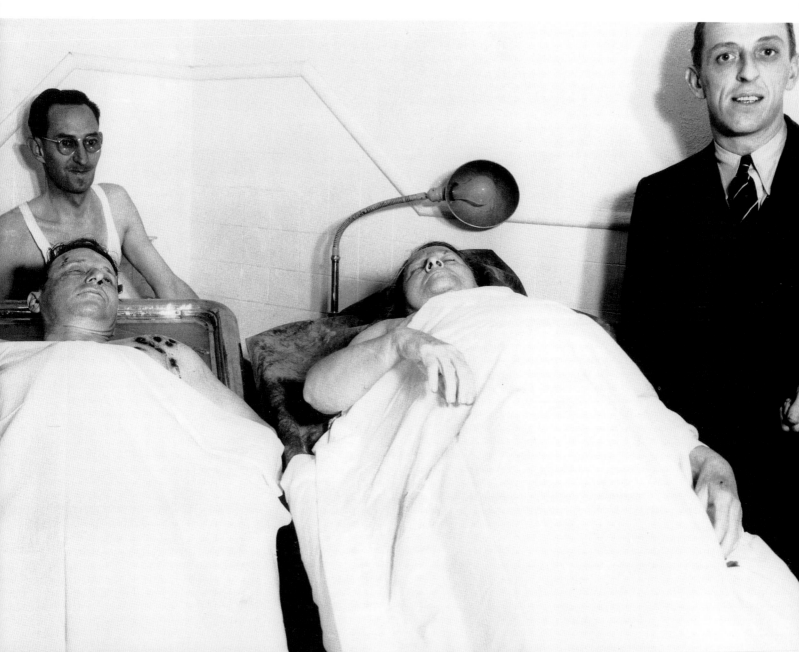

Machine Gun Kelly

Sometimes the legend has more substance than the man. This is the case with Machine Gun Kelly. His early years are an enigma. It is known that he was born George Kelly Barnes, but was it in Memphis or Chicago? Was it 1895 or 1897? Was he born into poverty or the son of an insurance executive? If the latter, it is instructive, for a story holds that young George caught his father having an affair. He confronted Dad with it, and by extortion secured a higher allowance and the use of the family car, which he used for bootlegging.

He enjoyed running booze, and after a brief stint in college and an aborted marriage, he turned to it full-time. In the late 1920s, now calling himself George R. Kelly, he met Kathryn Thorne, who had been employed as a manicurist and prostitute, and was recently widowed in a questionable suicide. She bought her new beau a machine gun and made him practice shooting walnuts off a fence. Legend has it that he got his nickname because he could

write his name on a wall with the gun, but Kathryn may have concocted this. She handed out the spent cartridges from his target practice as souvenirs from Machine Gun Kelly, who was, she claimed, busy elsewhere robbing banks. It has been suggested that he was more likely off somewhere on a drunk.

After serving time in Leavenworth in the early '30s for selling hooch on an Indian reservation, he did embark, verifiably, on a series of bank robberies, but Kathryn, now his wife, decided that kidnapping might be the way to go. Their victim was Charles Urschel, a wealthy Oklahoma oilman. When they got the $200,000 ransom, they set him free, although Kathryn had wanted to off him.

The couple was finally found in Memphis in 1933. Once again, accounts differ. One has local policemen breaking in on the wife and husband, who drops his gun on his foot. A second has FBI agents bursting in on them, and Kelly saying, "Don't shoot, G-men, don't shoot!" In any case, Kathryn was undoubtedly tormented during the trial when her husband was referred to as Pop Gun Kelly.

He died in prison in 1954. Kathryn, who always blamed her husband for "this terrible mess," was set free a few years later.

During the Oklahoma City kidnapping trial, famed "bad boy" Machine Gun Kelly looks like he can't believe what he's gotten himself into. Or was it really that his lovely wife, Kathryn, got him into it? The little lady herself, at left, looks like she can't figure out how she got mixed up with this loser. She told him over and over they should have killed the guy.

Dutch Schultz

Like anyone else who ever knew him, I disliked him intensely," said Willie Sutton. The famed bankheister was referring to Arthur Flegenheimer, who was born in the Bronx in 1902 to German Jews. His doting mother tried to bring him up to be a religious boy, but the grammar-school dropout followed more readily in the footsteps of his saloon-keeper father. Before too long, Arthur had recast himself as Dutch Schultz because "it was short enough to fit in the headlines."

Schultz knew that there was easy money to be made in a thirsty Prohibition era, and after some mentoring by the crime genius Arnold Rothstein, he was on his way to earning the title Beer Baron of the Bronx. He got there by being very rough—he took on Mad Dog Coll and Legs Diamond—very mean (the notorious madam Polly Adler said, "He seemed to have no more warmth or need for human companionship than a machine") and so cheap that, according to Lucky Luciano, "Here was a guy with a couple of million bucks and he dressed like a pig . . . His big deal was buyin' a newspaper for two cents so he could read all about himself." Nobody liked the Dutchman, but everyone feared him.

Schultz was such an abhorrent figure that he ended up an anachronism. As Prohibition persisted, most other gangs formed partnerships, but he was unable to take advantage of these lucrative pacts. As a freelancer moving beyond the beer biz, ruthlessly taking over the huge-dough Harlem numbers racket and building a slot machine empire to boot, Schultz was putting himself in peril and, in the end, his virulence and aggression proved too much for other criminal kingpins.

In 1935 he became the primary focus of New York special prosecutor Thomas E. Dewey. When his income became threatened, Schultz told a recently formed national crime syndicate, "Dewey's gotta go! He's my nemesis. I'm hitting him myself and in 48 hours." The syndicate, fearing public reprisal, instead sent hit men to the Palace Chop House and Tavern in Newark, where Schultz was shot by Charles "the Bug" Workman. Schultz survived into the next day in the hospital. Toward the end, he began to ramble incoherently and the police

kept a stenographer at his bedside to glean useful information. They found nothing, but William S. Burroughs, the author of *Naked Lunch,* later used the bizarrely poetic transcript for a literary project.

Even in death, Schultz was held in disdain. Only four floral tributes were sent to his grave, an obvious gangland insult.

In August 1935, Schultz is all smiles after beating a tax rap in Malone, N.Y. Two months later he is on his deathbed in Newark City Hospital.

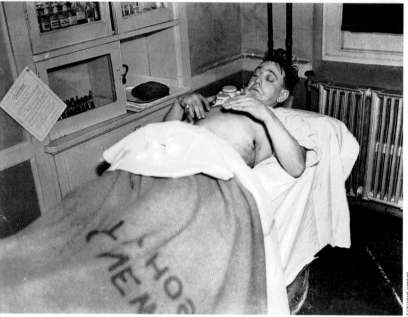

Al Capone

H e is one of the most famous people of the 20th century, a gangster of international prominence whose name evokes the very worst of gangland mayhem. Yet there are misconceptions about Al Capone. He was never in the Mafia, and dealt with it only tangentially. Neither did Capone possess a great criminal mind. He was cunning, certainly, and not without intelligence, but in essence he was but a sadistic savage who used brute strength to achieve his ends. It is possible that his name might simply have faded away had not a smash-hit television show, *The Untouchables,* indelibly revived his persona in 1959.

Alphonse Capone was born into a large family in Brooklyn on January 17, 1899, the son of a barber and a seamstress. He quit school at age 14 after he knocked down a female teacher and was in turn beaten by the principal. He was already a big kid, a veteran of countless street brawls who had joined his first gang, the Bim Booms, when he was 11. Lucky Luciano was also a member, and both boys moved on to become Five Pointers. There they met Johnny Torrio, a lieutenant who was smart as well as street-smart, a leader who let his minions do the dirty work. Johnny would get Capone a lot of jobs, both in New York and elsewhere, and it was one of the earliest that provided Capone with his immortal nickname. Thanks to Johnny, Al was working at the Harvard Inn one night when he insulted a woman at the bar. Her brother happened to be there, and he slashed Capone three times with a knife. The press would later dub him Scarface, although his intimates called him Snorky.

In 1919, Capone joined Torrio in Chicago, where Terrible Johnny had gone to oversee matters for his uncle, the crime lord Big Jim Colosimo. The city at that time was a den of bribery. Capone was ostensibly assigned to low-level chores, but what Torrio had in mind all along took place on May 11 when someone—Capone?—rubbed out Colosimo. Torrio, now the top dog, named Capone as his right-hand man. Big Al would specialize in bootlegging and its attendant homicides.

Torrio's operation was impressive, but on Chicago's North Side was another rough outfit, an Irish and Polish mob run by Dion O'Bannion, who para-

The New York Times

36 LIFE MOBSTERS AND GANGS

On a visit to Florida circa 1930, Capone shows he isn't camera-shy. Once Torrio (inset, in 1939) had a bellyful, he was heard to say, "It's all yours, Al."

doxically was a flower enthusiast. Torrio liked to keep squabbling to a minimum, so he sliced the city into sectors for different gangs. Capone, however, was difficult to keep in tow, always trespassing, even though he had more money than he knew what to do with. For him there was never enough. Finally, in November 1924, three of Scarface's men strolled into O'Bannion's florist shop and shot him dead.

Revenge was inevitable, and two months later, Johnny Torrio stopped five bullets. He somehow survived but he had had enough, and handed the reins to Capone. So Big Al was Numero Uno, but O'Bannion's successor, the volatile Hymie Weiss, vowed to kill Capone. Chicago, as Lucky Luciano said from the relative calm of New York, was "a damned crazy place! Nobody's safe in the streets!"

The tommy gun, a most effective tool, had become the weapon of choice. In September 1926, Capone was in the Hawthorne Coffee Shop, next to his HQ in Cicero, the nearby city that was his fiefdom. Weiss sent 10 cars to the hotel. Each stopped outside, and the passengers emptied their guns. More than 5,000 bullets were fired and Capone, though unhurt, was rattled. Was anywhere safe for him? Well, at least he could get rid of one demon. Before year's end, Hymie Weiss was gunned down.

The St. Valentine's Massacre in Chicago happened not far from where Dillinger was shot. Bugs Moran was the primary target, but he was late.

As Capone said, "You can get a lot more done with a kind word and a gun, than with a kind word alone."

The world looked on Chicago as an abattoir, but the coup de théâtre was yet to come. On February 14, 1929, five Capone goons, three disguised as cops, entered a garage on North Clark. They lined up seven of Bugs Moran's men and machine-gunned them to death; Bugs himself was running late. Though Scarface was in Florida at the time, Moran opined, "Only Capone kills like that!" The St. Valentine's Day Massacre spurred President Hoover to order a get-tough edict on crime, specifically Capone, who killed perhaps a thousand before he was through.

That moment came as a result of his thickheadedness. Capone never paid

U.S. marshals guard Capone on October 24, 1931, his sentencing day. Right: On November 16, 1939, he is taken from the Harrisburg, Pa., railway station en route to being released, a madly grinning ghost of his former fearsome self.

any income tax, and the IRS nailed him. In 1931, Judge James H. Wilkerson said, "Eleven years!" *The New York Times* said, "The fat man's face went dark and the ugly scar went white." He served most of his time in Alcatraz, before being judged insane and released in 1939. He had contracted syphilis long ago from one of his whores, and it destroyed him. Capone spent the rest of his years in Florida, dying of a brain hemorrhage on January 25, 1947. After visiting him there not long before the end, his former accountant, Jake "Greasy Thumb" Guzik, said to newsmen, "Al? He's as nutty as a fruitcake."

THE MOLLS

Every guy had a doll, and she wasn't always wifey. Sometimes, controlling the moll situation was nearly as difficult, dicey and dangerous as pulling a job.

GAY ORLOVA

Appearing every inch a femme fatale in the 1932 edition of *Earl Carroll's Vanities* in New York City, Orlova (above) was Lucky Luciano's main squeeze. The showgirl would have appreciated her legacy to entertainment: For a performance as the Orlova-based alcoholic moll in the classic 1948 film *Key Largo,* Claire Trevor won an Oscar for Best Supporting Actress.

AP

KIKI ROBERTS

"She may have some of my husband's attentions," said long-suffering Alice "Mrs. Legs" Diamond of showgirl Marion "Kiki" Roberts, "but I have the man." Would that she had kept him home, for it was by following Kiki's trail on the night of December 18, 1931, that Diamond's killers found their victim. The next year, Kiki eased her grief with a Cuban vacation. Here she mugs for the camera alongside one of Havana's finest.

TEXAS GUINAN

"Hello, sucker!" was the signature greeting of the flamboyant hostess from Waco at the several New York speakeasies she was involved with during Prohibition. Bankrolled by gangster friends, notably Larry Fay and then Owney Madden, she got rich and lived fast, going through perhaps three husbands—no one's sure— and lots of lovers in her 49 years.

VIRGINIA HILL

She dated (to use the euphemism) Frank Nitti, Joe Adonis, Frank Costello and many, many others. The Mistress of the Mob was star of the 1951 Kefauver hearings, where she attributed her high standing with the guys directly to her talent in the sack. She truly loved Bugsy Siegel but was absent the night he was murdered in her living room. Hill committed suicide in 1966.

LIZ RENAY

Renay's résumé: Wife of seven, lover of scores (including DiMaggio, she says), stripper, actress in wacky flicks including *Spies A-Go-Go* and John Waters's *Desperate Living,* great-grandma, songwriter, painter of nudes, author of memoirs (including *My First 2,000 Men*), friend of mobsters (most prominently Mickey Cohen), Vegas legend

JANICE DRAKE

According to the New York *Daily News,* the former Miss New Jersey's husband "took an open approach to marriage and didn't mind if his wife dined with other men." These included, in 1957, the Lord High Executioner of Murder, Inc., Albert Anastasia. The day after supping with Janice, Al got clipped in the barbershop. Janice, too, was killed, beside gangster Little Augie Pisano, in '59.

THE WOMEN OF SAM'S CLUB

Chicago, that toddlin' town, gave nothing away to New York when it came to notorious men living notoriously. Al Capone caught the disease that would wreck him from one of his prostitutes, and Sam Giancana dated famously. Judith Exner, left, was Sam's pal, which might have been okay had she not also dallied with U.S. President John F. Kennedy. Whether there was pillow talk or not, after rumors arose that the mob may have been involved in a plot to kill Fidel Castro, or even in JFK's assassination, the Exner link took on a new dimension. Longtime Giancana girlfriend Phyllis McGuire (below, right), along with her songbird sisters, is squired to a London nightclub by Momo in the early '60s. In '65 she had to tell a grand jury what she knew—or didn't—about the mob.

N.Y. Daily News

THE WIFE'S LOT ...

... was not an easy one. Since we know that Al Capone died syphilitic, we can presume that his relationship with spouse Mae underwent trials. Speaking of which: While a moll could jump ship in bad times, the gangster's wife was expected to sit stoically by her man in the courtroom. The most dedicated of the wives went a step further, visiting hubby in prison. Here, in 1937, Mae uses her fur as a shield against paparazzi after dropping in on Big Al at Alcatraz. If there was a silver lining, it was that life was a lot calmer at Casa Capone.

Bettmann/Corbis

THE MOB IN AMERICA

The coast-to-coast syndicate that ruled crime for most of the 20th century was much more than just the Mafia. It was an overarching, ruthless and extremely deadly corporation.

The United States branch of the Mafia has never been pure. Well, obviously: They kill people. But we mean pure in the Sicilian, Black Hand, omerta sense. These elements were damaged in shipping, and the mob's structure and traditions in the U.S. have always been knockoffs of the original rather than authentic hand-me-downs. Part of the problem for the Sicilian Mafia in trying to export its operation was America's troublesome melting-pot ideal. In a land of liberty, Irish, Jews, blacks and others were just as free as Italians and Sicilians to try their luck at organized crime. As we have seen in the testimony of gangster Arnold Rothstein, whose grand scheme for a crime syndicate was the blueprint for the Jewish-Italian collaboration of Meyer Lansky and Lucky Luciano, any self-respecting red-white-and-blue criminal considered himself an American first, an ethnic second. Certainly not all American mafiosi agreed with this view, especially at the beginning, but in relatively short order the underworld became an assimilated culture.

Rothstein was a realist. Veteran of a Jewish gang in New York City that had grown powerful and then been crushed by a larger, mixed-race-but-principally-Italian gang, he realized, as did Lansky and Luciano, that talent, execution, cooperation and size were vital to criminal success. From the start, these men envisioned and pursued alliances across cultural bounds. At the start, they were opposed in their efforts. Sicilian mafiosi arriving in New York, New Orleans and other port cities tried to establish just the type of close-knit and omnipotent organizations they remembered fondly from home. They learned quickly that things were different. Other criminals wanted in on the action, and just as shocking, American authorities were not content to allow Sicilians to enforce among their own. Back in Sicily, the mafia *was* the law, but here, if a mafioso violated an American statute—say, he shook down a Sicilian neighbor—he might be arrested and punished for it. This was a new and disappointing state of affairs to the Mafia.

Still, one man above others, the fearsome Vito Cascio Ferro, dreamed of Sicilian rule over American crime. But prison terms in Italy and bullets in America conspired to write *finito* to Don Vito's quest as soon as it was begun. By the early '30s it was clear the U.S. mob would be a new thing with new rules. It would be, for better and worse, a very-few-holds-barred syndicate.

The syndicate was nationwide, baby. To be able to strut his stuff as boss of Chicago, Sam Giancana had to be thoroughly mobbed-up. And was he ever.

Don Vito Cascio Ferro: Exporting the Mafia

Just what was the Black Hand? Neither a secret society nor an oracular curse, the Black Hand as practiced by mafiosi in Sicily and Italy since the 18th century, and as exported to America during a flood of Italian emigration beginning in the 1890s, was a scummy extortion racket inflicted on one's own people. The victims—from struggling Sicilian vegetable sellers to the most rich and famous Italian Americans—would receive a note ("Most Gentle Mr. Silvani: Hoping you will be so good as to send me $2,000 if your life is dear to you . . ."), the memo stamped with *La Mano Nera.* When opera star Enrico Caruso visited New York, he would be threatened with a dosage of lye in his vino, and for years he forked over as much as a tenth of his considerable salary to Black Handers. Uptown, in Harlem's Little Italy, Ignatius "Lupo the Wolf" Lupo was a demonic exponent of the Black Hand, killing more than 20 at his "murder stable" to keep his message clear, while netting thousands of dollars in the bargain.

Back in the old country, a more patrician practitioner of Black Hand–style extortion was Vito Cascio Ferro, as close to a Boss of Bosses as the Honored Society ever had. On the lam for kidnapping in 1899, he visited America, liked what he saw and returned to Sicily with some new ideas. Principal among them was the notion that he or a minion should be overlord of crime in America, and should seek to organize it after the Old World model.

When Benito Mussolini took power in Italy in 1922, he cracked down on the Mafia. Perhaps a thousand Italian mobsters fled to the U.S. in the '20s, most of them thrilled to do so because Prohibition had made bootlegging a far more lucrative career than Black Hand extortion. Don Vito sent many soldiers over, and in 1927 asked Salvatore Maranzano to go to New York City with the aim of organizing crime—first there, then everywhere.

"Little Caesar" Maranzano met with immediate resistance. Giuseppe "Joe the Boss" Masseria, who had fled a murder charge in Sicily back in 1903, was already entrenched at the head of a mob that

Opposite: The Don of Dons, Ferro poses for a portrait with his loving nephew (but, of course, a gun is present). He sent his surrogate Maranzano (above) to America for easy pickings. The pickings were anything but, thanks to Masseria (below).

included promising lieutenants Frank Costello, Vito Genovese, Carlo Gambino, Joe Adonis, Albert Anastasia and above all Lucky Luciano. Maranzano and Masseria went to war, and as dozens of mobsters fell in battle over many months, some younger gang members came to see the intramural killing as unnecessary, distracting and senseless, particularly as Irish and Jewish gangsters were keeping their eyes on the prize. Furthermore, these new kids on the Italian block had scant reverence for the kiss-my-ring notions of "honor" and even omerta—the Mafia law against ratting one another out—insisted upon by Masseria, Maranzano and Ferro. "Mustache Petes," these Young Turks called the old guard, as they drifted further from their leaders and closer to an alliance.

Luciano became leader of this dissident faction, which included not only his friends from Masseria's gang but Tommy Gagliano and Tommy Lucchese from Maranzano's side. When the Young Turks flipped a coin for which mustache to shave first, Masseria lost. In April 1931, Luciano spent a nice afternoon in a Coney Island restaurant playing cards with Joe the Boss, then politely excused himself. Adonis, Genovese, Anastasia and Bugsy Siegel burst in and opened fire. When the cops arrived, Masseria was well dead and Lucky was well relieved—though wholly ignorant of what had occurred. "I was in the can taking a leak," he explained to the law. "I always take a long leak."

Maranzano tried to suck in Luciano and Co., making Lucky his top associate. But then he named himself *capo di tutti i capi*—Boss of Bosses—of this new invention of his, Cosa Nostra (Our Thing). Luciano realized there was another step to be taken. His thinking accelerated when he learned that Maranzano had hired Mad Dog Coll to eliminate Costello, Genovese, Adonis, Lucky himself and even his old Five Pointers sidekick, Al Capone. Luciano struck first, and Maranzano was assassinated on September 10, 1931. Back in Sicily, Mussolini already had Ferro firmly locked away on a counterfeiting charge, and the influence of the Mustache Petes on the American mob was no more. Lucky Luciano had a clean slate upon which to draw not the Cosa Nostra, but his own Cosa Nuova.

Lucky Luciano

The most important crime figure of the 20th century—and arguably of all time—was born Salvatore Lucania in 1896 in Sicily, and immigrated to America with his family in 1906. He was barely off the boat before he was pinched for shoplifting, the first of dozens of arrests. In 1915, as an underling in the Five Points Gang, he was pulled in for dealing drugs. When he didn't rat out his cronies during six months in stir, he began his ascent in the netherworld of criminality.

His nickname, Lucky, may have derived from his skill at cards. With his gambling profits and his Five Points lucre, he set up his own operation,

Charles Luciano
Alias Lucky
Waldorf Astoria Hotel
Crime Compulsory Prostitution
Age 39   5 · 9½
Wt. 156   Medium build
Hair Blk.   Eyes Brown
Color White   Comp. dark
Born New York City
Occupation Bookmaker
Arrest 4/16/36
Officer Kennedy
G.J. Sqd.

Having been extradited from Hot Springs, Ark., on prostitution charges in 1936, Luciano is greeted in New York by an escort of 48 police officers and detectives.

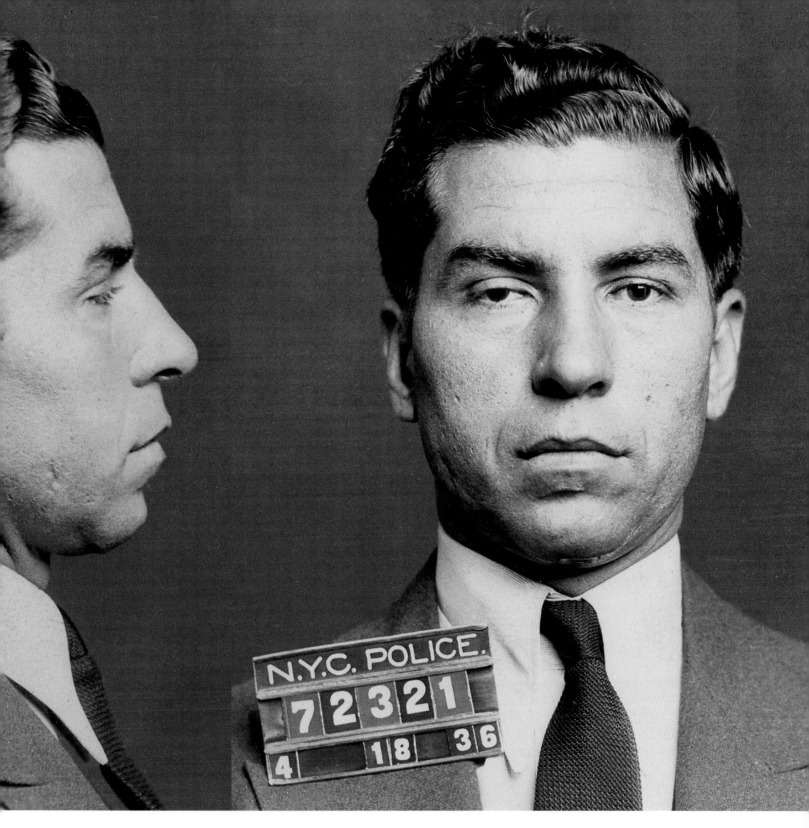

N.Y.C. POLICE.
7 2 3 2 1
4   18   36

wherein he and his hoods shook down bordellos. By the mid-'20s he ran the entire New York prostitution racket, with 5,000 ladies in his employ. Unfortunately for Lucky, he liked to sample the merchandise, and he repeatedly came down with sexually transmitted diseases.

It was around then that Luciano became Joe Masseria's right-hand man, running his gambling,

booze and drug operations. Things were just ducky for Lucky. He dressed swank—silk underwear, bespoke suits—and tore around town in sleek automobiles. He lived in a deluxe suite at the Waldorf. He was making more than a million clams a year.

Still, there might be an even better way. He happened into an old acquaintance, a Jewish guy he had met years before, Meyer Lansky. Luciano told

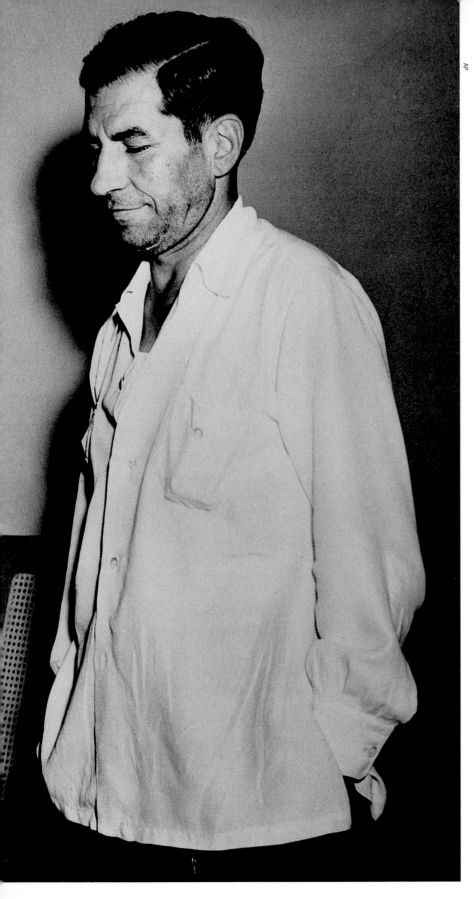

Above, in the Tiscornia immigration camp on February 24, 1947, Luciano wears a guayabera, an informal Cuban shirt, as he awaits deportation from that island nation to Italy. The U.S. government, worried about his proximity, had pressured Cuba to evict him. At right, under guard in Genoa.

him some of his ideas, big ideas, like setting up a vast, streamlined operation that would benefit everyone—at least the criminals—and that would eliminate the endless internecine squalls. Lansky, who had also profited from early classes in philosophy with the master, Arnold Rothstein, concurred implicitly, setting the stage for a close, decades-long relationship based on trust and cemented by phenomenal earnings.

Luciano was clever enough to know that to make an omelette, you've got to break a few yeggs. When Masseria and Salvatore Maranzano waged their messy, protracted gang war, Luciano arranged their twin demises in '31.

All along, Luciano had been fine-tuning his relationships with the younger crowd. Now, with the inflexible Mustache Petes—and soon, other, unpredictable sorts like Legs Diamond and Dutch Schultz—out of the way, the path was cleared for a lean, mean operation, a syndicate with Lansky, Frank Costello, Louis Lepke Buchalter and Lucky's longtime amigo Joe Adonis on the board of directors. Luciano, of course, would rule over the cartel.

In 1935, New York City special prosecutor Thomas E. Dewey turned his focus fully to the boss. "The vice industry, since Luciano took over," said Dewey, "is highly organized and operates with businesslike precision." After a doozy of a trial, Luciano was sentenced to 30 to 50 years.

Even behind bars, Lucky pulled the strings, but life in the ancient Dannemora, N.Y., prison was a far cry from the glossy Gotham nightclub circuit.

Then fate intervened. In 1942 the Navy asked Luciano to help beef up wartime security on the New York waterfront. Luciano ran the longshoremen's union, so sabotage on the docks was instantly snuffed out. There was even a rumor that Luciano greased the way for the Allied invasion of Sicily. In any case, in February 1946 he was released from jail and deported to Italy. He tried to settle in Cuba, where he was host to such guests as Lansky, Costello and Bugsy Siegel, but the authorities there eventually booted him off the island. He settled in Naples, where he lived a life of luxury and kept his hand in the running of aliens and drugs into America. In January 1962 the vice lord had a heart attack at the Naples airport and died. He had been under surveillance and was about to be arrested, said authorities, for smuggling $150,000,000 worth of heroin into the U.S. in the previous 10 years. Lucky never rested till he rested in peace.

At a party in Rome in 1949, Luciano turns on the charm. In his beautiful Naples villa (right), he relaxes with his beloved pet miniature pinscher in the mid-1950s.

Frank Costello

Of central importance to the rise of organized crime in the United States was an Italian immigrant who toted a gun but preferred to get things done the old-fashioned way—with a whispered promise and a pocketful of hush money. Thus did Frank Costello attain the title Prime Minister of the Underworld.

In 1895, four-year-old Francesco Castiglia immigrated to Harlem, where his Calabrian parents set up a small grocery store. A tough kid, he put a black handkerchief over his face and robbed his family's landlady when he was 14. He hung out with Owney Madden's nasty gang, the Gophers, and was arrested a number of times while in his teens. In 1915 he was sentenced to a year in jail for carrying a con-

During the Kefauver hearings, the nation watches with growing fascination as the publicity-shy Costello exercises his fingers while invoking the Fifth. Offscreen (top), he considers the advice of attorney George Wolf.

cealed weapon. By that time, he called himself Frank Costello, the surname a telling choice with its Irish connotations. This was one Italian who was not straitened by ethnic exclusivity. He had a profitable relationship with Big Bill Dwyer. He married a Jewish woman named Loretta Geigerman, and a few years later went into a legit business with Harry Horowitz. The company produced—get this—Kewpie dolls, used as prizes for the punchboard craze. (Hey, he made 80 grand in less than a year.)

Costello was a man who had a lot of "partners," but none of them more significant than two he met as a boy, Lucky Luciano and Meyer Lansky. He teamed with Luciano on booze, slot machines and gambling. With Lansky he set up the Havana operation. As important as his gangland connections was the slew of cops, politicos and judges—he called them "my boys"—with whom he curried favor, and vice versa. There were, just for one example, widespread rumors of an "understanding" with J. Edgar Hoover. Costello was, in sum, the link between the mob and the so-called straights.

The cool-headed Prime Minister was invaluable, a crime titan, and everything was humming along, until the late '40s. Luciano had been deported, and the ruthless Vito Genovese was setting sights, as in gunsights, on the Luciano family top spot. Then, in the early '50s the Kefauver committee held its televised hearings into crime. Costello testified but refused to have his face onscreen. So the camera showed only his hands, in a bizarre finger rumba set to the tune of his raspy voice (reportedly adopted by Brando for his *Godfather* role), which was endlessly taking the Fifth. For one who had dwelled in relative anonymity, he had become overnight the symbol of the American mobster. In 1952 he drew a sentence of 18 months for contempt, then another five years were tagged on for income tax evasion.

Costello's power was dwindling. His public presence made deals much harder to put over, and Genovese was breathing down his neck. On May 2, 1957, Genovese sent Vincent "the Chin" Gigante to kill him. Costello was in his apartment building when Gigante cried, "This is for you, Frank," and fired from point-blank range. Costello heard the voice and turned his head, and the bullet merely scraped his temple. But he got the message and before long opted for retirement, which he seemed to thoroughly enjoy. In 1973, he died in his sleep.

Leonard McCombe

Above, Costello relaxes with a cigarette in New York City during the spring of 1949. The scene at left recalls a less tranquil moment in the mob boss's life as Vincent "the Chin" Gigante looks out from behind bars in New York on August 20, 1957.

In Las Vegas, Lansky stands before the Thunderbird Hotel, which he packaged for the syndicate. Decades earlier, he stood still in New York City for a different sort of photo.

Hy Peskin/Getty

Meyer Lansky

The story has it that the face of crime was forever altered on October 24, 1918, when the diminutive 16-year-old Meyer Lansky was on his way home from work. He lived with his family, which had immigrated to New York a few years earlier. Meyer had been a good student, never a problem, and his father had secured a promising tool-and-die job for the boy.

Suddenly Meyer heard screams from a deserted building. Inside he discovered a woman and a teenage boy, both naked. The woman was being roughed up by another young fellow, her pimp, who was furious because she was doling out sexual favors gratis. When the boy tried to fight back, the pimp beat him and threw him to the ground. The scene infuriated Meyer, who pulled a wrench from his tool kit and applied it to the pimp's head. Shortly, the cops came along and hauled them all off. The case came to naught, and as Meyer was leaving the courtroom, the pimp introduced himself. He was Salvatore Lucania, later to be known as Lucky Luciano. The boy who was with the whore was Benjamin Siegel, soon to be tagged as Bugsy.

Lansky and Siegel became fast friends and soon set up a thriving crap game. They impressed Little Augie Orgen enough that, for a cut, he gave them money and protection. Everything was jake for a year, then Lansky decided to get his own tough guys rather than fork over so much to Orgen. The Bugs and Meyer Mob started in the early '20s with shakedowns, car thefts, hijacking and rum-running. The goons they hired were the seeds of Murder, Inc., the frightening contract killers.

It wasn't long before Lansky ran into Lucky Luciano again. They talked for hours and agreed that they would be better off working together.

Henceforth, for example, Bugsy's goniffs would steal a car, Meyer's henchmen would change its looks and serial number, and Lucky's smoothies would sell it to the suckers. Here was the germination of the crime syndicate.

At meetings of crime bigwigs in the late 1920s and early '30s, a hierarchy was taking form, and Lansky was the primary architect. He had a tremendous knack for keeping everyone happy and in line. As Luciano once remarked, "I used to tell Lansky that he may've had a Jewish mother, but someplace he must've been wet-nursed by a Sicilian." He also said that the Little Man, as Lansky was called, was one of the toughest guys—physically toughest—he ever knew, "and that takes in Albert Anastasia or any of them Brooklyn hoodlums or anybody anyone can think of."

Lansky was farsighted and always kept an eye on the big picture. In 1936 he arranged exclusive gambling rights in Havana, an irresistible market sitting right off the U.S. coast. He always understood that the take from a legitimately run casino was infinitely preferable to the ephemeral income from a clip joint. Lansky, through Siegel, set up the syndicate's operations on the West Coast in the '30s and a decade later in Las Vegas. He ultimately expanded the operation into South America and Asia. As an FBI agent put it, "He would have been chairman of the board of General Motors if he'd gone into legitimate business."

For much of the time, the Little Man stayed out of the limelight. In 1950-51, however, a far-reaching Senate crime investigation headed by Senator Estes Kefauver, spread Lansky's name across the nation. Lansky was never put away, but in 1970, perhaps fearing tax-evasion charges, he tried to relocate to Israel. That nation ousted him as a "danger to public safety," and returned him to the States. The tax charges didn't stick; it's rumored that he parlayed his influence in the highest echelons of government. But even if he wasn't in the pen, Lansky's final years were wracked by physical pain. The man who said of the mob, "We're bigger than U.S. Steel," died of natural causes in 1983.

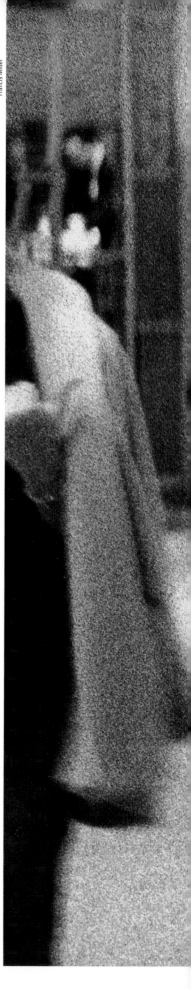

Lansky is hauled into the Dade County, Fla., clink on a drugs charge in 1970. Things were better in 1958 in Cuba. As LIFE wrote at the time, "No. 1 gambler and organizer of the Havana boom, Meyer Lansky leaves Riviera casino with girl and satchel reported to have contained $200,000 from cashier's office."

The New York Times

Bugsy Siegel

Benjamin Siegel was very hands-on in the evolution of organized crime. A scion of poverty, he was born to Russian Jewish immigrants in Brooklyn in 1906. While a boy, he preyed on pushcart vendors. If they didn't pony up, he doused their carts with kerosene and torched them. As a teen, he and Meyer Lansky ran a gang. Lansky said he "was young but very brave. His big problem was that he was always ready to rush in first and shoot—to act without thinking."

That low flash point gave him his nickname, the mere mention of which set him off. Bugsy had a serious yen for violence. Even in later years, when he was a crime royal, he liked to be in on the dirty deed, as with the Joe Masseria killing and countless others. When Luciano and Lansky launched their syndicate in the early '30s, they needed muscle to carry out their plans, so Lansky created Murder, Inc., a pack of killers siphoned mainly from Jewish gangs, and handed the reins to Siegel. Murder, Inc., was strictly "professional." They didn't work for outsiders nor were they sicced on politicians; it would attract too much attention. As Siegel once said, allaying a businessman's fears, "We only kill each other." The group was later run by Louis Lepke Buchalter and the dreaded Albert Anastasia,

and boasted triggermen like Abe "Kid Twist" Reles and Albert "Tick-Tock" Tannenbaum. Murder, Inc., marked the inception of "contract" killing, in which the gunmen have no link to the victim and so are difficult to catch. Of the 500 or so murders committed nationwide, Lansky, Luciano and/or Frank

Bugsy sits for a portrait in 1940, the ne plus ultra of the celebrity mobster, with de rigueur cigar and pinkie ring. Seven years later, he is still a syndicate cover boy, but unfortunately those are his florid gunshot wounds that blend in so perfectly with Virginia Hill's floral living room motif. She was conveniently in Europe at the time of the shooting. Inset: his bête noire, the Flamingo, in 1946.

Costello probably signed off on every one.

By the mid-'30s, things were plenty hot for Siegel. He had made a ton of enemies and had frequent run-ins with the police (though he would never serve time). Luciano and Lansky were tiring of his "acting without thinking," so they sent him to California to goose the rackets out there and infiltrate the Hollywood scene. Jack Dragna was the big wheel on the coast at the time, and while he was none too happy when Siegel arrived, he managed to control his ire when he received this minatory missive from Luciano: "Ben is coming West for the good of his health and [the] health of all of us."

Bugsy was perfect for his new job. As a Jew he was able to mingle comfortably with the Hollywood moguls. And he wasn't your garden-variety psychopath, but was charming, witty and handsome, with blue eyes and black hair. He couldn't keep his paws off the ladies, but then, most of them seemed to like the arrangement.

Siegel rented a mansion and was shown the ropes by boyhood pal George Raft, the veteran portrayer of screen gangsters. Raft introduced Bugsy to the ravishing Countess Dorothy diFrasso. Reputedly, she once took Siegel to her estate in Italy, where he met Hermann Goering and Joseph Goebbels. They bugged Siegel in some way, and the contessa had to beg him not to kill the Nazis.

In the mid-'40s, Bugsy, acting on his own idea or at the behest of Lansky, carved out a plan for a lavish casino in the innocuous desert town of Las Vegas, Nevada. The Flamingo was a fiasco from the start, beset particularly by cost overruns—the latter mostly from Bugsy's skimming syndicate money, which Virginia stashed in Europe. Reckless endeavor. Finally, even Lansky agreed that Siegel had to be hit. On June 20, 1947, he was reading in Virginia's living room when shells from an Army carbine burst through the window and ripped into Bugsy. They found his left eye in the next room.

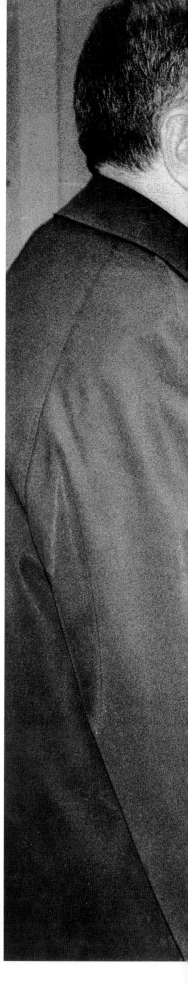

The Five Families

Just before getting himself zotzed in 1931, Salvatore Maranzano was helpful enough to organize his New York City crime kingdom into five "families," each of which had a "boss," to wit Lucky Luciano, Joe Bonanno, Vincent and Phil Mangano, Joe Profaci and Tom Gagliano. Maranzano was to be Boss of Bosses, but suddenly he was dead, thanks to Lucky and Co. Luciano then surveyed what Maranzano had built—with its commission of patriarchs making decisions that governed the overall operation, with New York being the nation's capital of crime—and liked what he saw. For reasons of diplomacy and perhaps longevity, he erased the Boss of Bosses post (while retaining it de facto), then rubber-stamped the rest of Maranzano's architecture.

It is in Mafia blood to angle for power, but for a remarkably long time Luciano's syndicate was something like stable. Consider that Bonanno headed his eponymous family until 1968; the Manganos

On October 25, 1957, acting on behalf of Carlo Gambino, someone (good guess: the Gallo boys) pumped 10 shots into Albert Anastasia as he sat in a midtown Manhattan tonsorial parlor. Right: Gambino himself, now the don, is cuffed in 1970.

and Gagliano ruled for two decades what would become known as the Gambino and Lucchese families; that Luciano, in and out of jail, would exert control until handing off to Frank Costello in 1946; and that Profaci would stay in power for 31 years before Joe Colombo took over that clan. The family structure was sound.

But the Mafia family itself was dysfunctional. Even in the early years, soldiers and capos alike were being beaten up, nicked or whacked by other mafiosi. Joe Bananas tried to bump off Carlo Gambino and Tommy Lucchese, Albert Anastasia killed Phil Mangano, etc. And once the jailed Luciano and other originals were out of circulation, all bets—and pretenses of honor—were off.

It would be foolhardy to try to make sense out of the multitudinous machinations and murders that occurred in the American Mafia during the

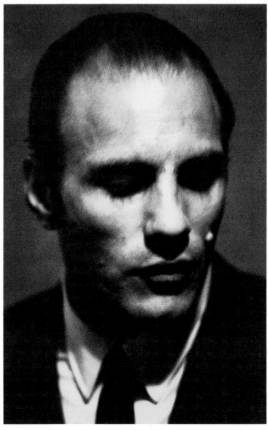

heyday of its power, which lasted from 1931 until the mid-1980s. Generalizations are more useful here, as are star turns.

Generalization: Mob power, emanating from New York, was nationwide, even global. Bugsy Siegel, based in L.A. and Las Vegas, was a mobster, and Meyer Lansky in Havana was a mobster. They were not of the five families, but they were always in touch. Lucky Luciano in prison, then in Italy, was ever a mobster. Sam Giancana in Chicago was not allowed to be arm's-length in his relationship to New York, as Al Capone had once been.

Another generalization is that there was never one top-dog boss, although some were more powerful than others. After Luciano was put away, it became every family for itself. The Bonannos, Genoveses (formerly Lucianos) and Gambinos (originally Manganos, then Anastasias) have each been strongest in one era or another, depending on who had just been sent to the pen or to the cemetery.

Star turns: Leading the Bonanno family we find, for several years before his untimely death in 1979, Carmine Galante. In what began as the Profaci fam-

As youngsters in the Profaci/Colombo clan, Carmine Persico (top, being booked in 1951 at age 17) and Crazy Joey Gallo (left, in a Brooklyn court in 1961) belonged to rival factions. Years later, in the early '70s, Persico got the don's job, and Crazy Joey got himself killed.

ily we see not only the eight-year tenure of Joe Colombo but, from the 1970s to 1996, that of Carmine Persico. In the legacy extending from Tom Gagliano are the names Tommy "Three Finger Brown" Lucchese (head from 1953 to 1967) and also that of naturalist Anthony "Tony Ducks" Corallo (1974 to 1986).

There are few that are un-famous—and many infamous—in the branches of the Genovese and Gambino trees. Luciano bequeathed to Costello who was succeeded by Vito Genovese and, in later generations, "Fat Tony" Salerno and Vincent "the Chin" Gigante. Mangano was followed by Anastasia and

Gambino, who was trailed by "Big Paulie" Castellano and the Dapper Don himself, John Gotti.

In all of this, there was a star of stars: Carlo Gambino. From 1957 to 1976 he transformed his family into the ultimate criminal organization. He was—he is—the godfather.

As a young man, Carlo soldiered for both Joe Masseria and Salvatore Maranzano before enlisting in the Young Turks. He and his brothers-in-law, Peter and Paul Castellano, were in the Mangano family when the brothers Mangano were killed in 1951 (well, Vince's body was never found; conclusions may be drawn). The notorious killer Albert Anas-

Shortly after Joe Colombo posed for this picture with his sons, he was gunned down at an Italian Unity Day rally. He lingered in a coma for seven years before dying in 1978.

The cops took Vito Genovese's picture in 1945; he became head of his family 12 years later. In 1979, Bonanno chief Carmine Galante (top) and associate Leonardo Coppola had a bad meal at Joe and Mary's Italian restaurant in Brooklyn.

tasia took over, and you could have received long odds that the unassuming Carlo would arrange to have his boss eliminated. But had you made the wager, you would have been handsomely paid. Gambino then helped set up the dangerous Genovese. A tip to the feds led to a drug bust, and Vito was sent upriver for 15 years. By 1957, Gambino, starting a two-decade run as don, was suddenly the most powerful mafioso in the U.S.

As such, he sought to keep interfamily strife to a minimum (though he did put out the successful contract on Joe Colombo in 1971). His strategies worked remarkably well for a remarkably long time, and Carlo Gambino lived out his 74 years naturally, dying in 1976 and handing the reins to in-law Paul Castellano. That would be a fatal mistake, but more about that when we get to John Gotti.

Gambino had been at the Apalachin Conference in 1957. Of course he had. Everyone who was anyone had been there: Gambino, Castellano, Genovese, Galante, Santo Trafficante, Joes Bonanno and Profaci and 60 other dons from around the world. It was held at Joseph Barbara's estate in New York state for the purpose of formalizing new structures and strictures within the mob.

A couple of local police officers noticed some suspicious characters booking into Broome County motels. The cops drifted up to the Barbara spread one afternoon and started taking down license-plate numbers. They were noticed by the mobsters, who fled into the woods. Chase was given, the mafiosi sweating into their sharp-pointed collars. "It looked like a meeting of George Rafts," Sgt. Edgar D. Croswell told *The New York Times* the following day. Several arrests were made, and much information was gleaned.

Until that day—November 14, 1957—J. Edgar Hoover's FBI had denied the existence of an organized crime syndicate. Now, the cat was out of the bag, the scales were off the eyes, the truth was set free. What had been happening since 1931 was clear, and what would go on for years—decades—to come, was frighteningly apparent.

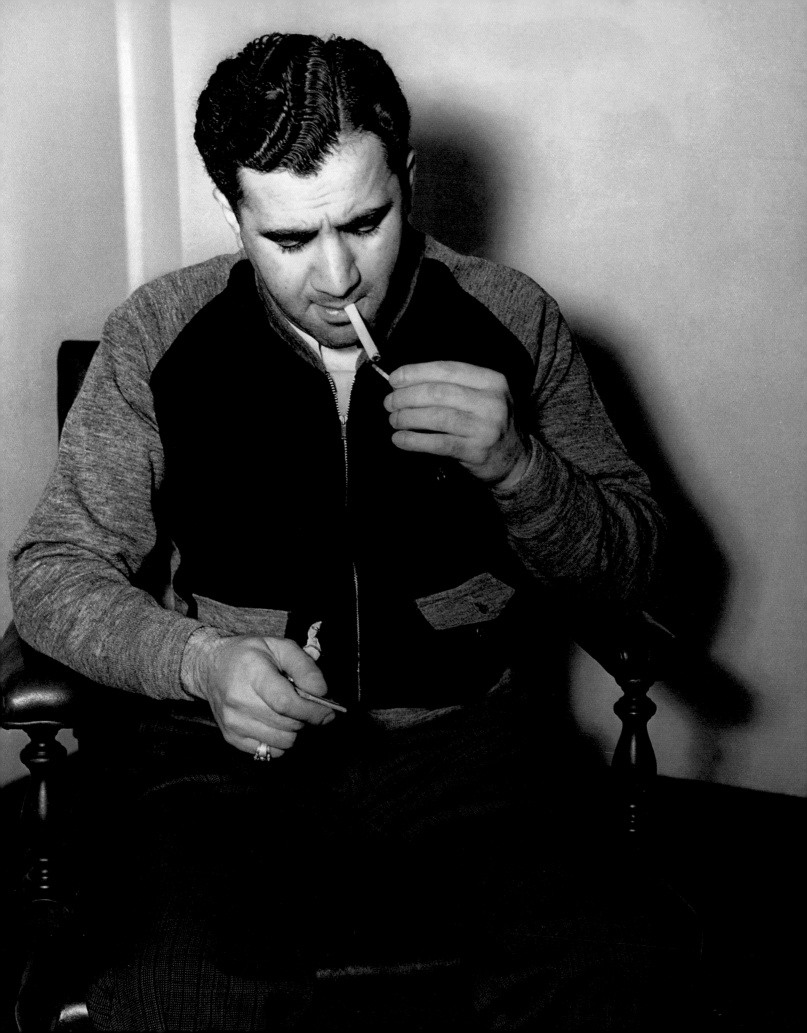

THE SNITCHES

The furtive rodentia to which they are often likened are rats. Nevertheless, these informants have played a vital role in the fight against organized crime.

ABE RELES

When he started singing in the Brooklyn D.A.'s office (opposite) in 1940, Murder, Inc.'s Kid Twist Reles didn't stop for two weeks. He recalled who, where, when and why about scores of murders. Reles sent four guys to the chair, including Louis Lepke Buchalter. In '41 the canary crashed when he "fell" from his heavily guarded hotel room.

JIMMY FRATIANNO

The Weasel, shielded at a 1981 appearance before the Pennsylvania Crime Commission by bulletproof glass and a black bag, knew all and spilled all—in court, in his 1981 book *The Last Mafioso,* and on *60 Minutes.* When asked on the program if he had been a good killer, Fratianno said modestly, "Some people are a little better than others."

ANA CUMPANAS

One of the most famous of all stool pigeons, she was born in Romania and came to the U.S. in 1914. In '34, calling herself Anna Sage, she ran a brothel in Gary, Ind., and consequently was facing deportation proceedings. For cash and the FBI's aid in preventing her being booted, she tipped the feds that she and a friend would be going to a movie in Chicago with Public Enemy No. 1 John Dillinger. They would recognize them by her garb. She was the notorious Lady in Red.

ARLYNE BRICKMAN

Growing up in Manhattan's Lower East Side, Arlyne didn't have the usual little-girl dreams. She wanted to be a moll one day, like the legendary Virginia Hill. After a failed marriage, she spent time as a call girl, then fell in with a Genovese family small-timer. When their numbers business got busted, she turned, and eventually wore a wire for several law enforcement agencies. Brickman testified at the trial that put Carmine Persico away in 1986.

SAMMY GRAVANO

Whether folks thought John Gotti was a misunderstood credit to society or a homicidal beast, there was unanimity of opinion that the guy who ratted him out in 1992, right-hand man Salvatore "Sammy Bull" Gravano (above, unbuttoning his silk jacket), was clearly a lower form of life. The Dapper Don (his silk jacket already unbuttoned) at least showed some dignity on his way to a prison grave. And we know they used to be good friends, because Sammy said he and John watched the Gotti-ordered Paul Castellano hit together.

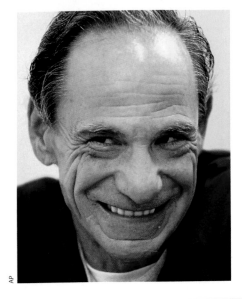

HENRY HILL

Having scuttled for years on the fringes of the Lucchese family, involving himself in cocaine, car theft, sports fixing and a half-million-dollar heist at JFK Airport, Hill was to prove useful when the FBI urged him to spill. Hill did, not only under oath but to author Nicholas Pileggi for *Wiseguy,* which became the film *GoodFellas* (Ray Liotta played Henry). After years in the Witness Protection Program, Hill dropped out. That he and fellow fink Arlyne Brickman chose to travel in the open air shows that threats of payback ain't what they used to be.

THE VITO GENOVESE FAMILY

THE GAETANO LUCCHESE FAMILY

JOSEPH VALACHI

His career reached all the way back to Maranzano's Cosa Nostra. Within the Luciano family he ran afoul of powerful Vito Genovese, and did the unthinkable: He flipped. No mobster had ever violated omerta so flagrantly as Valachi. And if his testimony before a Senate subcommittee in 1963 didn't tell the feds anything they didn't already know about the Mafia family tree, it transfixed—and shocked—the American TV audience. Don Vito put a $100,000 bounty on Joe's head, but Valachi died of a heart attack in 1971.

AP

RETRIBUTION...

...is a concern when you drop a dime on gangsters. Eddie O'Hare was a shyster lawyer in Chitown who with Al Capone's help made a lot of dough on a dog track they turned into Sportsman's Park horse-racing track. In return, O'Hare told the IRS how they could get the info on Scarface that would send him away. Anytime Artful Eddie felt put upon, he went snitch. On November 8, 1939, he paid the piper (left). A footnote: His son Butch, the Navy's first WWII ace, was shot down in 1943. The great Chicago airport is named after him.

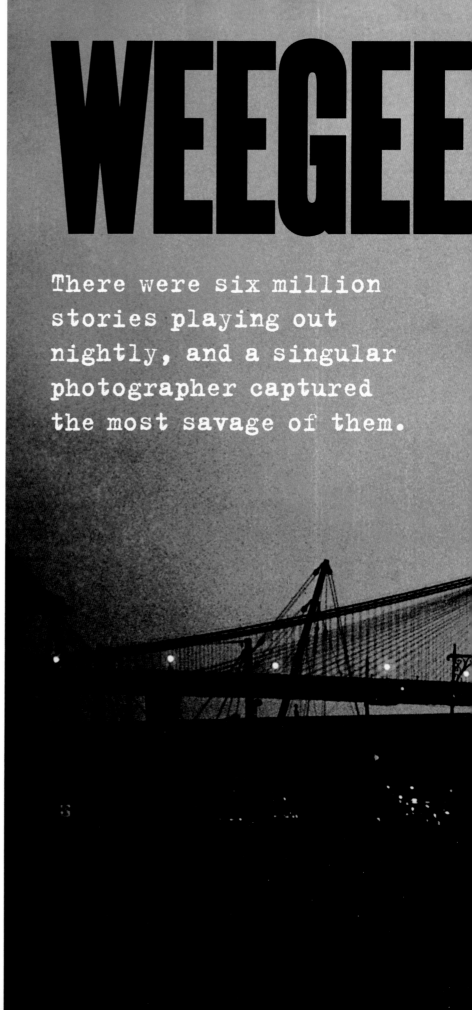

WEEGEE

There were six million
stories playing out
nightly, and a singular
photographer captured
the most savage of them.

Avedon and high fashion. Capa and war. Weegee and rubouts. These photographers were such definitive masters of their milieus that they shaped how we saw and reacted to a subject. In the case of Weegee, he took us where we feared to tread—onto the blood-soaked mean streets, into the noir. From 1930 to 1947, the New York demimonde that would come to be known as the Naked City was chronicled by an extraordinary shooter armed with a Speed Graphic camera and Compur flash unit.

His formal name was Usher H. Fellig, born in Austria in 1899. The family immigrated to the United States when the boy was 10, and settled in the tenements of New York City's Lower East Side. Usher—now Arthur—had a hard-bitten youth. He was on his own by age 18, working odd jobs, sleeping in flophouses in the Bowery for 25 cents a night. He loved music, and at one point scratched together a few shekels playing fiddle in a silent-movie theater. "I loved playing on the emotions of the audience," he once wrote. "I suppose my fiddle-playing was a subconscious kind of training for my future in photography."

Whether the name "Weegee" was a nod to his days as a squeegee-wielding darkroom technician

All photographs: ICP/Getty

'S NAKED CITY

at *The New York Times* in the 1920s or a tribute to his Ouija-like ability to know where the action was and beat all others to a crime scene, it was his professional calling card from the first. But it did not represent the full byline of his choosing. He stamped the back of each print CREDIT PHOTO BY WEEGEE THE FAMOUS, and he wasn't kidding.

Weegee was as grand a self-promoter as photography has ever known, but he worked very hard at his job and was established as a shooter by the mid-1930s. He would go to bed at sunrise, sleep all day (unless awakened by a police-alarm hookup at the head of his bed) and then travel the black streets in his Chevrolet, looking for trouble or anything interesting. His contacts included cops, firemen, bartenders, barflies, ambulance drivers and stool pigeons. The trunk of his car served as a darkroom, and photos taken between midnight and five a.m. would be in the evening editions.

"Looking back on the years of Murder, Inc., I find I used up 10 press cameras, five cars and every night

20 cigars and 20 cups of coffee," he reminisced in 1961. He chased after lowlifes, celebrities and, on regular occasion, gangland victims. His unique eye made life after dark seem simultaneously surreal and all too real, and while he was diligent in recording what actually happened, he always filtered a scene through the Weegeean sensibility. One of his most famous photographs, which appeared in *PM* on October 9, 1941, is telling. Weegee was in Brooklyn as kids from P.S. 143 in the Williamsburg section gathered around a car, ogling the corpse of a just-slain gangland figure. Peter Mancuso had been shot twice by an unknown gunman as he sat parked at a traffic light. In the photograph, Mancuso's aunt has arrived on the scene and is registering her grief. Meanwhile, the woman's son—the dead man's cousin—is pushing the girl in front of him in order to get a look at his late relative. The image is perfectly composed, fantastically lighted and filled with amazing timing, luck and coincidence. It's an impossible picture: a Weegee.

In 1941 in Brooklyn, the schoolchildren from P.S. 143 revel as Peter Mancuso's aunt recoils. In '36 in Manhattan, gangster Dominick Didato, a.k.a. Terry Burns, is down and out on Elizabeth Street. According to the cops, he was killed for horning in on Lucky Luciano's racket— never a good idea.

Few places in Gotham were safe when the operatives of Murder, Inc., plus a thousand unincorporated lowlifes, went strolling after dark. In the late 1930s and early '40s, a bocce court becomes a crime scene, as does a brick-paved alley, then Rosco's owner is offed in a bar.

Crime-scene voyeurism was prime-time entertainment in the most depressed neighborhoods of Depression-era Manhattan. Opposite: In Hell's Kitchen on the West Side, apartment dwellers watch cops clean up a murder. It's a similar scene up on East 106th Street, where a rooftop turns into the first balcony as detectives fingerprint murdered store owner Joseph Gallichio.

Though Weegee was a talented photog, some folks just didn't want their picture taken. Among them: Henry Rosen and Harvey Stemmer (top left, with hankies), who are charged in 1945 with bribing Brooklyn College basketball players; apprentice auto thief Harold Horn, 16, in the squad car in 1941; and Brooklynites Charles Sodokoff and Arthur Webber, in the van in '42.

Life at the station. In January 1941, gunman Anthony Esposito (above) is prepped for a lineup after a brutal bit of business that will become known as the Battle of Fifth Avenue, in which a businessman and police officer were killed. Left: an unidentified bruno in bracelets that same year. Right: The curtain's about to go up at a lineup in 1944.

NEW YORK IS A FRIENDLY TOWN

Weegee's first book of photographs, *Naked City,* published in 1945, inspired the 1948 movie—on which Weegee served as a consultant—as well as the subsequent television series. With this multi-media success, Weegee popped nationwide and quickly forsook New York for Tinseltown. He quit the hard life of dusk-to-dawn and began making "art photography." He continued in this vein until his death in 1968.

The later work, though much of it is commend-able and all of it is interesting—it's by Weegee, and that's enough said—does not serve as his legacy. The night-shift archive does, and he knew it. "I had got the famous pictures of a violent era, the pictures that all the great papers with all their resources couldn't get, and had to buy from me," he once said. "For me, crime had paid—in a very lush way . . . And in shooting these pictures, I had also pho-tographed the soul of the city I knew and loved."

Weegee did feel warmly toward the wormy Apple, but when the chance came to be gone, he was. His ticket out was *The Naked City,* a headline attraction in '48, even over such as Tex Beneke and Martin & Lewis. No more makeshift darkrooms for Weegee. He was running for daylight.

Cops, pols and G-men like our friend with the tommy gun view crime-busting as a righteous crusade. Their ranks include geniuses, grandstanders—and many who are a mix.

THE LAWMEN

JOSEPH PETROSINO

A native of Salerno, he was New York's first Italian American detective. Formed in 1905, his "Italian Branch" (left), an elite undercover squad, caught 500 Black Handers. Petrosino chased Sicilian Mafia chief Vito Ferro during that man's visit to the U.S., but paid dearly. When the brave policeman went to Sicily to gather info on the mob in '09, Ferro had him executed.

ELIOT NESS

He was hired by the Department of Justice in 1929 to run its Chicago booze patrol, with a special eye out for Al Capone. Although he and his nine-man Untouchables (at right, he gives two a lift) harried Scarface, it fell to the IRS to bust him for taxes. Ness went on to clean up the corrupt Cleveland police force, but a mayoralty bid in '47 failed. His 1957 book led to the hit TV show, which linked him forever to Capone.

Brown Brothers (2)

Cleveland Public Library; Inset: Bettmann/Corbis

J. EDGAR HOOVER

The most important lawman in American history, the Top Cop (above, in '35) headed the FBI for 48 years till his death in 1972 at age 77. Over the years, his prickly personality often hindered, and questions abound concerning his "What Mafia?" stance, but he took over an agency in disrepute and willed it into a world-class crime-fighting conglomerate.

ROBERT F. KENNEDY

Bobby (left) made his reputation in the late 1950s as chief counsel for a Senate committee investigating corruption in organized labor. Teamsters boss Jimmy Hoffa (with RFK) was wholly uncooperative in his testimony; "You can't embarrass me, Bob!" was among his more polite ripostes. Hoffa, jailed in the 1960s for jury tampering and fraud, was pardoned by Richard Nixon in 1971. In '75, he went missing—forever.

RUDOLPH W. GIULIANI

In the '80s, LIFE asked a prominent gangster whether
U.S. Attorney Giuliani was really putting the heat on.
He grudgingly replied, "Yeah, he's tough. Plenty tough."
Indeed. He had 4,152 convictions against only 25 losses.
Here, in '88 with the parole board's Benjamin Bear and
Sen. Al D'Amato, he displays crack they purchased incognito.

SHOWBOATING...

. . . is a hallmark of the successful bust. Since the beginning
of crime, cops have held sacred the "perp walk," where
mugs are paraded before the press en route to booking.
NYC mayor Fiorello LaGuardia never missed a photo op,
and in 1934 he celebrates a smashed slot-machine ring.
It surely was galling for the world's Bugsys and Mad Dogs to
see a pip-squeak called the Little Flower showing them up.

THE MYTHOLOGY
OF MOBSTERS AND GANGSTERS

The world of film is one of artifice, and the theater of crime plays out backstage. They converge in a hazy hybrid: Gangland, U.S.A.

Ever since they started dimming the lights, crime has been elemental to the American cinema. *The Great Train Robbery* from 1903 is based on a Hole in the Wall Gang holdup. Audiences shrieked when a man pointed a gun at the camera and fired. It was thrilling stuff, the most popular movie of its time. The early "organized" gangs in movies were confined to the Old West, which, on celluloid, was a never-never land of cattlemen vs. farmers, of gunslingers who could make a thimble dance. In 1930, when Daryl F. Zanuck announced that Warner Bros. was going to make films that sprang from the headlines, gangster movies exploded onto the screen. *Scarface, Little Caesar, The Public Enemy,* guns blazing, bodies flying, cars screeching around the corner in a vivid departure from the photographed plays that most movies had been.

At the time, gangsters were everywhere, even in the hinterlands. How did Bonnie and Clyde and Dillinger know about gats and getaway cars? At least some of their notions came from the big screen. When Dillinger was shot, he had just finished watching Clark Gable play a gangster. Why, out in Texas, did the future Kathryn Kelly gift her beau with a machine gun and make him practice? She had to get the idea somewhere. And where did the

actors and designers get their inspirations from, for the fashions, cars, and argot? The movies made countless expressions part of the national idiom. The interplay between reel and real life became so intoxicating that Hollywood had to be constrained for a while. Rather than being appalled by Edward G. Robinson's Rico, some folks wanted to *be* Rico.

World War II moved the action drama to exotic locales for a while, and then the soldiers came home, harder and sometimes disillusioned; films went noir for a spell. The '50s followed, with the acrid McCarthy hearings about the enemy in our midst. The time was ripe for gangsters redux, only with cheaper and more lurid thugs. In the 1960s and '70s, color films became the standard, bringing a reality and éclat that were meat and drink for directors of serious intent. These auteurs gave us *Bonnie and Clyde* and the *Godfather* series, with gangsters and mobsters who were more intimate, more inviting than ever. Life imitated art which had imitated life, as many of today's made men memorized words and gestures of Marlon Brando and Al Pacino. James Gandolfini's Tony Soprano has a shrink. Of course. Frank Costello was in therapy long ago.

What, then, is the distinction between movie gangsters and real ones? What is, really, a gangster? The distinction isn't merely blurred, it's invisible.

James Cagney burst into stardom in 1931's *The Public Enemy*. Opposite: the final shot of *The Great Train Robbery*.

Wallace Beery (right) gets things off to a feisty start in 1930 with **The Big House**, one of the first in a string of gangster classics. Above, the one and only Cagney is going to the chair in 1938's **Angels with Dirty Faces**. Priest Pat O'Brien has asked the tough guy to make believe he's scared, so that the kids who idolize him will think he's a coward. Think he goes along with it? Below: It won't be long before Edward G. Robinson in **Little Caesar** (1930) asks himself, "Is this the end of Rico?"

Paul Muni in **Scarface** (1932)

Enough actors have portrayed Al Capone to fill a dermatologist's waiting room. De Niro's stint in *The Untouchables* was shorter than his cigar, but as usual he lit up the screen. Director Brian De Palma updated the 1932 *Scarface* with a Cuban gangster in 1983. Steiger and Gazzara are always potent.

Ben Gazzara in **Capone** (1975)

Al Pacino in **Scarface** (1983)

Robert De Niro in **The Untouchables** (1987)

Rod Steiger in **Al Capone** (1959)

Francis Ford Coppola's **The Godfather** (1972) teemed with memorable performances. Marlon Brando (opposite) led the way. Many of the gangsters discussed in this book have been the subjects of movies. Clockwise from above: Warren Oates captures the demons and style of **Dillinger** ('73); Faye Dunaway and Warren Beatty click in '67's **Bonnie and Clyde**; Lurene Tuttle takes aim in **Ma Barker's Killer Brood** ('60); Mickey Rooney leans on Carolyn Jones in **Baby Face Nelson** ('57).

Anthony Neste

Globe Photos

Kobal Collection

Joe Pesci is a plenty convincing hothead, and never more so than in Martin Scorsese's **GoodFellas** (1990). The boys, including Robert De Niro and Ray Liotta, look very much like they wish he'd put that gun away. In **Road to Perdition** (2002), Paul Newman chalks up one more sterling performance.

The allure of the crime drama remains as strong as ever. *Perdition* was a solid hit, and cable TV's **The Sopranos** is nothing less than a phenomenon. The patriarch, Tony, played to brilliant effect by James Gandolfini, is in the classic mold of a man who does horrid things yet is adored by the viewer. Scorsese's next film, **Gangs of New York**, takes him—and us—back to the days of the brutal Five Points mobs. Here, Daniel Day-Lewis (left) and Leo DiCaprio agree to disagree.

GEORGE RAFT

When Bugsy Siegel was hauled into court in July 1944 on charges of making book in a glitzy Hollywood eatery, his old pal George Raft testified in his behalf. Some say that Siegel based his look on Raft's, others that Raft modeled his screen persona after Bugsy (or maybe Joe Adonis).

FRANK SINATRA

Whether or not Old Blue Eyes owed the comeback to his godfather, à la *The Godfather,* he did have pals in the mob, including Paul Castellano (far left), Carlo Gambino (third from right) and Jimmy Fratianno (second from right), who pose with him in Tarrytown, N.Y., in 1976. When Fratianno turned Weasel, he told of Sinatra's Mafia ties.

GUNS & GLITTER

Fame cozies up to fame like a moth to a flame, and stars of the real world have long found underworld stars alluring. If they flutter too close, they get singed.

Getty

Bettmann/Corbis

LANA TURNER

The screen star and her lowlife lover Johnny Stompanato, back from a smashing holiday in Mexico, are greeted in March 1958 by Lana's daughter, Cheryl Crane. Two weeks later, the 14-year-old stabbed him to death with a butcher knife in Lana's bedroom. Justifiable homicide. Lana's next film, *Imitation of Life*, was her biggest hit ever. Cheryl later became a real-estate broker in Hawaii.

Czarek Sokolowski/AP

STEVEN SEAGAL

They oughta make it a movie: When 17 reputed Gambino members and associates were indicted in June 2002, allegations described an extortion scheme against action hero Seagal by his former producer.

THE CELEBRITY ORBIT...

... led to countless close encounters between the clean and the crooked. No one is saying that Chicago Cub Gabby Hartnett was mobbed up. But he's happy to sign a ball for Sonny Capone while making nice to Big Al in 1931. How'd Al score those seats?

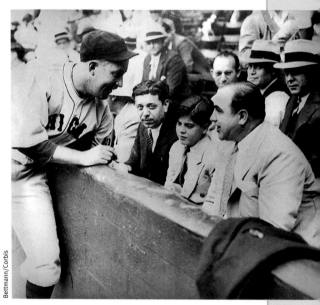

Bettmann/Corbis

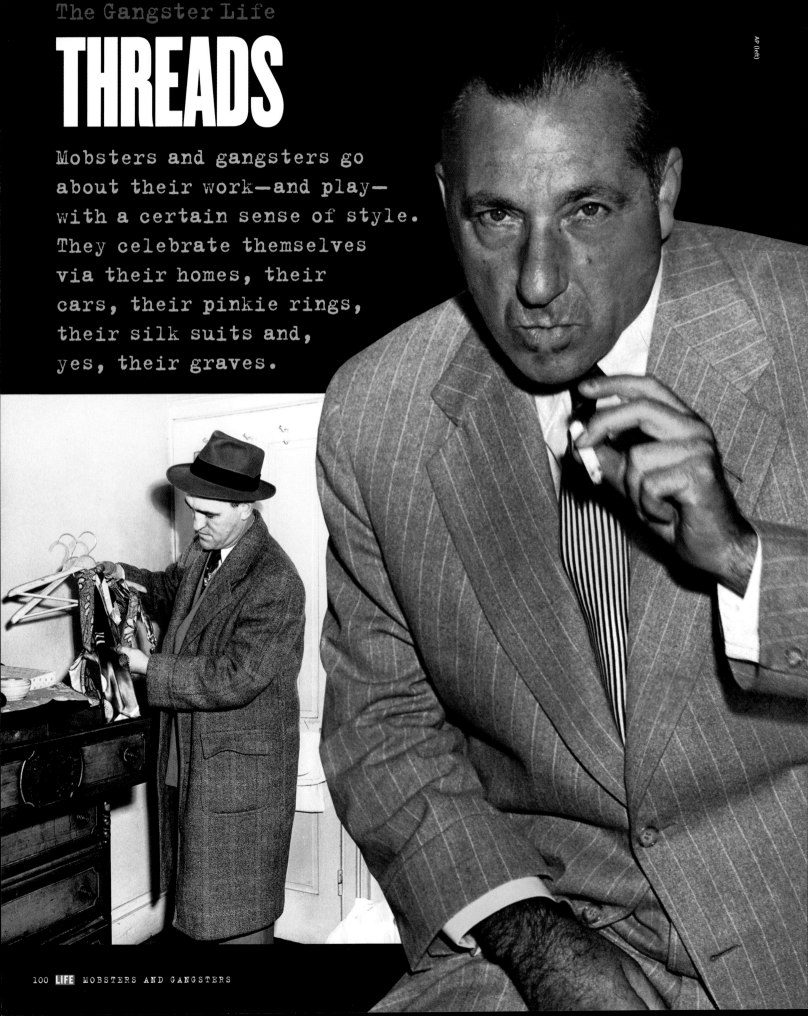

The Gangster Life

THREADS

Mobsters and gangsters go about their work—and play—with a certain sense of style. They celebrate themselves via their homes, their cars, their pinkie rings, their silk suits and, yes, their graves.

work to be done and image to be shown. Frank Costello (with cigarette), a dyed-in-the-worsted crime king, rivaled Bugsy Siegel for smoothoid supremacy in the golden age. Angler Al Capone set a bathrobe standard that George Raft could only aspire to. Feds check out bank robber Willie Sutton's wild neckties. In the modern era, there was the Dapper Don. His hair was perfect, his cravats electric, his stride strong: John Gotti.

DIGS

Two diametrically opposed strategies have always been operative in a criminal's choice of address. One is, I'm a big shot; fear my wealth and power. The other goes, I'm not what you think; leave me alone.

Top left: Carlo Gambino, an adherent of the Modest School of mob architecture, resided at 2230 Ocean Parkway in Brooklyn. (Observing family tradition, a later Gambino don, John Gotti, lived small in Queens.)

Left: Capone's crib in Miami let everyone know Big Al slept here. Above: An Italian-marble pool in this rococo mansion perfectly reflected Cincy bootlegger George Remus's style in the 1920s.

WHEELS

Being a wealthy guy, the organized criminal often has a car for work and one for the weekend. The latter is showy, full of pizzazz. The former is fast and bulletproof.

Al Capone's 1928 Caddy (top) was utilitarian: bulletproof side windows plus a rear "turret" window. Bank robber Willie Sutton's splendid Chevy led to his downfall in '52. Its battery went dead when he left the ignition switch on overnight. While recharging, he was nabbed. Kids analyze the evidence.

Places of relaxation—well, plotting and relaxation—become crime scenes. Top: Dutch Schultz loved Newark's Palace Chop House till he was killed there in 1935. Above: After an attempt on John Gotti's life in '89, cops are thick as thieves at his redoubt, the Bergin Hunt & Fish Club in Queens.

HANGOUTS

The home is where the wife and kids are kept on a daily basis. The nightclub or "hunt club" is where the boys convene just as regularly. Most of the fellows are happier out of the house.

UPRIVER

Given the choice, a gangster or mobster would like to consider the club his home away from home. Of course, he doesn't always get a choice. Many of the boys while away the hours in the hoosegow.

AP

Alcatraz, "the Rock," was a draconian host to 1,545 men from 1934–'63, among them Capone, Karpis, Kelly and the Birdman. It's now a magnet for Bay Area tourists. These other two are still open for business. Sing Sing, north of NYC, is seen at right in 1916. Note the grandeur married to austerity. In the city itself, this spartan cell in the Tombs was new in '41. Oh, well. You make your bed and you lie in it.

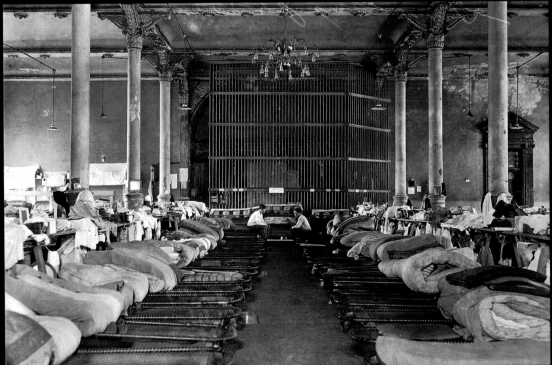

Underwood Archives

The Gangster Life
TOOLS OF THE TRADE

Heaters are an essential, and the organized criminal feels as warmly about his gun as a fisherman does his fly rod or a ballplayer his special glove. Explosives come in handy too.

Underwood Archives

N.Y. Daily News

Left: Ernie Bowen's mob, minoring in burglary and majoring in safecracking, pulled 100 jobs in the 1920s using this arsenal. (Ernie was snuffed by his partner in San Francisco in 1927.) Above: The Legs Diamond collection, which included bulletproof vests, pipe bombs and grenades, was seized by the law in Brooklyn in 1930.

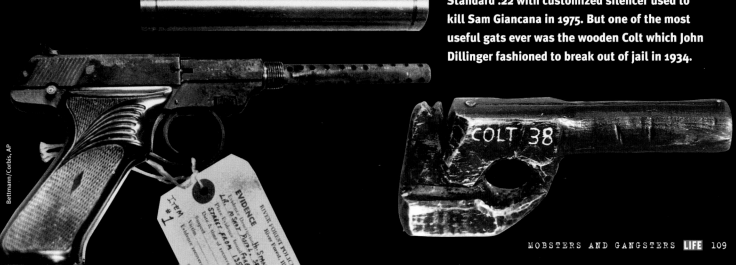

Guns could be truly impressive, like the High Standard .22 with customized silencer used to kill Sam Giancana in 1975. But one of the most useful gats ever was the wooden Colt which John Dillinger fashioned to break out of jail in 1934.

COLT 38

EVIDENCE

ITEM #1

David Rentas/N.Y. Post/Rex USA

Osmund Leviness/N.Y. Daily News

Globe Photos

SEND-OFFS

All things—good and bad—must come to an end.
Whether a gangster dies well before his time
or at the end of his natural term, his funeral
often reflects the outsize life he led.

Above, in an image out of a Bergman film, Mad Dog Coll's widow, sister and a few others gather in 1932 on an aptly dreary afternoon on East Tremont Ave. in the Bronx. Left, in 1962, Lucky Luciano's *arrivederci* in Naples sounds a more baroque note. For John Gotti's procession in 2002, an infinity of limos and bouquets files through Queens.

IN MEMORIAM

Through his tombstone
or tomb, the deceased is
able to make a final
statement. As with his
spats, club or moll, his
resting place shouts:
Here is a real gangster.

Clockwise from top: Capone may have died in Florida, but his survivors wanted him near the Windy City. They chose this edifice, perfectly capable of coping with drafts. Lucky Luciano (né Lucania) succumbed in Naples but is interred in Queens. When stoolie Kid Twist Reles died in 1941, also in Queens, a newspaper caption read: "A Dead Rat . . . a traitor even to the code of his kind."

AT HOME WITH MICKEY COHEN

In the Rat Pack Era, the guys and dolls were having a time: Sinatra swingin', Vegas sizzlin' and one brazen gangster struttin' his stuff.

You might suppose that a hoodlum would be shy about inviting famous photographers inside the gates to do a standard day-in-the-life shoot. You would be correct in your supposition—except in the case of Mickey Cohen, a flamboyant five-five fireplug who learned the Celebrity Gangster style from the master, Bugsy Siegel. Cohen was one of Siegel's guys when Bugsy got bopped in 1947, and he inherited his mentor's Los Angeles bookmaking enterprises. He immediately found himself in turf conflicts with fellow L.A. mobster Jack Dragna and other syndicate bosses, and would spend the rest of his life ducking. He survived at least five assassination attempts. A particularly near thing occurred when Dragna's goons detonated a pipe bomb in the basement of Cohen's L.A. home. A cement safe on the floor above took the brunt of the blow, and Mickey, wife LaVonne, dog Tuffy and a maid were all unharmed.

Dragna couldn't get Mickey but the feds could. They put him away twice, once for four years and once for 10, each time on a tax rap, never for the murders his mob was committing in California and Nevada. Upon each release, Mickey went right back to his extravagant, in-your-face lifestyle. He had casas in La-La Land (left) and in Vegas, and courted the press at each. They loved him for it, particularly in 1958 when he graciously shared love letters he had in his possession. They were from Lana "Sweater Girl" Turner to Mickey's late bodyguard, Johnny Stompanato, who had been offed on Good Friday by Turner's 14-year-old daughter, Cheryl Crane. In one of the all-time sensational incidents in the history of the Mickey Mouse Mafia, as L.A.'s wacky underworld was known, Cheryl heard her mom and Johnny arguing, grabbed a butcher knife from the kitchen and plunged it into Johnny's chest. Who bequeathed Mickey the letters is uncertain.

Mickey pronounced himself a reformed man upon his final release from the pen in 1972. Surely the Left Coast media lamented this, for Cohen had put on a smashing performance during the finger-snapping postwar years—as is seen on these pages.

Against considerable odds, Mickey Cohen died of natural causes in 1976 at the age of 62.

LIFE photographer Ed Clark visited Mickey and LaVonne at their Brentwood home (here and previous pages) for the 1950 story "Trouble in Los Angeles." The trouble was Mickey's, as cops were unfairly rousting him—his phrase—for having cursed at them. Mickey pleaded his case to LIFE's readers: "I take my oath on my mother, my wife and my dogs—and I'm very fond of my dogs—I ain't guilty of what they say about me."

Ed Clark (3)

In the City of Angels, Cohen cuts cards with business manager Mike Howard, and poses with a book and box given him by the Hebrew Committee of National Liberation (inscription on the box: TO A FELLOW FIGHTER FOR HEBREW FREEDOM). LaVonne knits and nicens up. "They have been married nine years," LIFE reported. "Mickey believes her maiden name was Brenf but isn't sure. Mrs. Cohen lives very inconspicuously, rarely accompanies Mickey and 'the boys' to Hollywood nightclubs." The week of LIFE's story, Mickey was due in court on an assault charge.

Ed Clark (4)

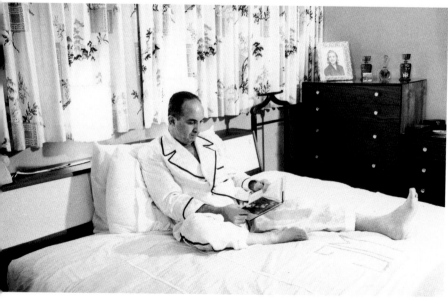

Gene Lester/Getty (5)

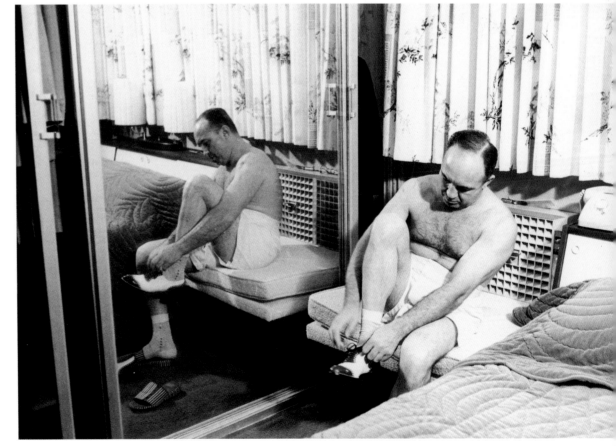

Photographer Gene Lester checked in with Mickey at his Las Vegas digs in the mid-'50s. The racketeer was back in business, fresh out of the can after four years on the first tax rap. He's clearly happy to see pooch Mickey Jr., and to trade prison issue for sportier threads. Fashion-plate Cohen had 200 suits tailor-made, at $300 per.

Proudly featured atop Mickey's wall of memories in Vegas is an outtake from the 1950 shoot that yielded a screaming-headlines portrait for LIFE. Cohen was instinctively provocative. Near his life's end, he campaigned for prison reform, of all things, and said he had inside dope on the whereabouts of kidnapped heiress Patty Hearst. He once told Mike Wallace: "I have killed no man that in the first place didn't deserve killing by the standards of our way of life." By any standard, Mickey Cohen was a piece of work.

THE MODERN GANGSTER

Long gone are the days and ways of Baby Face and Legs. The contemporary heistmeister is more human than Mad Dog. He's a man with a conscience who, in his retirement, may be found warning folks off the evil criminal life.

Willie Sutton

Ultrasmooth New Yorker Willie Sutton, a.k.a. "the Actor" and "Slick Willie," liked expensive clothes, disguises and banks. One of his victims once said Willie was so gentlemanly and adept, the experience of the robbery was like being at the movies. Sutton went about his robberies dressed as a cop or a maintenance man. He broke out of prison many more times than once, though one time he was foiled. He had hoped to escape by putting a homemade dummy (right) on his cot. A guard watched him labor on the model for several weeks, then told Willie to cut the nonsense. After Sutton was released from Attica State Prison on Christmas Eve, 1969, he finally went straight. He wrote books about his exploits and told his not-so-tall tales to television audiences via shows like Merv Griffin's. He died in 1980 at the age of 79.

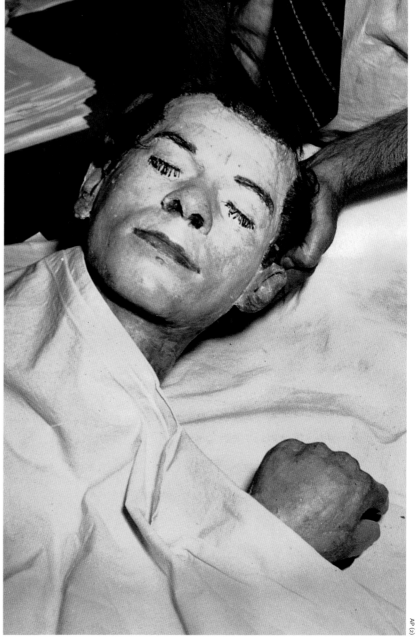

Murph the Surf

The snazzy Jack "Murph the Surf" Murphy leaves criminal court in New York City in 1964 after pleading innocent to jewelry theft (left). And this wasn't just any jewelry theft: He and a couple of other men lifted more than $400,000 worth of gems, including the 563-carat Star of India sapphire, from New York's Museum of Natural History. Murphy had, at that point in his life, traveled a twisty road from Florida beach bum and surfing champion to self-described gangster. The road would twist on: After being convicted of a caper so bold that it inspired a biopic starring Robert Conrad, Murph went away for a couple of years, then emerged and, shortly, was convicted of murdering two women. In all, he spent 20-plus years in Florida state prisons, where he found God and started to give back (below, in 1978, he counsels kids to avoid his wicked ways). After his release, Murph went on the Christian lecture circuit.

THE MODERN MOBSTER

Detroit no longer rules the car market, it's been ages since Ma Bell had phones to itself, and the mob doesn't own crime anymore. What's left of the syndicate is still illicitly inclined, but is facing a whole new ball game.

John Gotti

In life, he was known not only as the Dapper Don but also as the Teflon Don, because authorities had so much trouble finding a charge that would stick. In death—which came in the summer of 2002—he was referred to as the Last Don, because surely a man of his style, stature and power would never come again. John Gotti, who rose through the ranks in the Gambino family and then secured the top job by ordering a 1985 hit on boss Paul Castellano (below), came out of several traditions: the Godfather line, the Celebrity Gangster mold, the family man/ruthless killer continuum. He was finally done in by tape recordings and a turncoat, "Sammy Bull" Gravano, an erstwhile best friend and reliable triggerman. Gotti spent the last 10 of his 61 years in Marion Federal Penitentiary, then was entombed in a Queens cemetery where also rested Carlo Gambino, Joseph Profaci, Carmine Galante, Joe Colombo and Lucky Luciano. These guys left behind families with dwindling memberships and new pressures—from the law, from interlopers.

SPARKS

New Mobs

For the last few decades, immigration from Russia has been on the upswing. Among the newcomers are a lot of hardened criminals whom the KGB released from their prisons. Over here, they formed mobs, and found ready recruits among other needy Russians. These mobsters, latter-day Lucianos in their ecumenism, have established ties with the Sicilian Mafia and the Colombian cocaine cartel. At left, alleged Russian Mafia tsar Vyacheslav Kirillovich Ivankov is escorted from Brooklyn's Federal Office Building in 1995.

Above, in New York City in 1989, Benny Ong, a.k.a. Uncle Seven, shakes hands in Chinatown's Silver Palace. Ong ruled the Hip Sing Association—a powerful tong organization that used the Flying Dragons street gang as muscle—for 20 years until his death in 1994. The Chinese gangs are more isolated from the mainstream, and they mainly prey on their countrymen. They're throwbacks to the Sicilian Black Handers of a century ago.

CRIME DOES PAY

Afterword by Elmore Leonard

The picture was taken in Memphis, most likely during the summer of 1934, a few months before I turned nine. The ladies are my sister, Mickey, my mother and a family friend whose name I don't remember. The car, an Oakland, once made by General Motors, stands in the driveway of our home, which used to be on the corner of Poplar Pike and Crestmere Place. An office building now occupies the site. The picture might have been taken by my dad. He was with General Motors and kept getting promotions that moved us six times before I was nine: from New Orleans, where everyone in the family was born, to Dallas, to Oklahoma City and back to Dallas, to Detroit and then to Memphis for a couple of years before returning to Detroit in the fall of '34.

For several years, not too long ago, a 40-inch photostat blowup of the picture hung on a wall of my study in Birmingham, Mich. Next to it was a mounted newspaper photo, also blown up and grainy, of Buck Barrow—brother of outlaw hero Clyde Barrow—sitting in his undershirt, mortally wounded, in a field near Dexter, Iowa. Police and deputies, who shot him six times that day in July 1933, are all around him. We were in Memphis at the time.

A few years earlier, though, we were living in Dallas, where in 1930 Clyde Barrow first set eyes on Bonnie Parker, a little blond-haired waitress, 19, working hard to get by while her husband, Roy, was doing 99 years on a Texas prison farm. Meeting Clyde Barrow changed her life. They were not nearly as good-looking as Faye Dunaway and Warren Beatty, but were younger; Bonnie 23, Clyde 25, the day they were shot 187 times in an ambush near Gibsland, La., May 23, 1934.

I would guess that photo by the car in Memphis was taken not too long after, because by October of that year we were in Detroit and the Tigers were playing the Cards in the World Series.

But the most telling clue of all is my pose, foot on the running board and cap pistol aimed at the camera—not unlike the famous shot of Bonnie Parker holding a revolver against her hip, a cigar stub clamped in the corner of her mouth and one foot on the front bumper of a car bearing a 1933 Texas license plate. Faye Dunaway struck the same pose in the movie and it wasn't bad.

Looking for the original Memphis shot, I came across an earlier gun pose that lacks the swagger of the one on this page. I'm only about four in this one, wearing bib overalls and standing by our house in Oklahoma City. I'm wondering if maybe it was inspired by Charles "Pretty Boy" Floyd, who robbed banks in Ohio about that time. I don't suppose the outlaw would have to be local, though; John Dillinger was raising all kinds of hell in those days. So was George "Baby Face" Nelson, Vincent "Mad Dog" Coll, Ma Barker and her boys . . . I seem to have liked guns then, a lot, and yet I don't own one now.

Another early photo that puzzles me, taken when I was four or five, has me sitting in a toy airplane, a kind that you pedal to make it go, dressed in a cowboy outfit—the hat, cowhide chaps and pistol. It might indicate a conflict of interests or maybe a desire to have it both ways: influenced by Ken Maynard and Hoot Gibson in western serials as well as Smilin' Jack, the pilot in the funnies. Ken and Hoot must have moved me in a more positive way, for 20 years later I was writing westerns.

But what is most significant to me is the apparent effect of that 1930s outlaw period on the main body of my work. I seem to be dealing with characters in contemporary situations who closely resemble those desperadoes: down-home killers who grew up on an oil lease in Oklahoma, served time in a Texas prison or came out of the Florida Glades to a life of crime. There's a character in my novel *Killshot* whose ambition is to rob a bank in every state of the union except Alaska: "He had thirty-seven states to go but was young." About Clyde Barrow's age.

I don't know what the appeal is about outlaws, but it's a fascination that can afford you a good living. I'm glad I put my foot on that running board back in 1934 and aimed a cap pistol at the camera.